Big Mouth

Vogue Williams

Big Mouth

HarperCollins*Publishers*

HarperCollins*Publishers*
1 London Bridge Street
London SE1 9GF

www.harpercollins.co.uk

HarperCollins*Publishers*
Macken House, 39/40 Mayor Street Upper
Dublin 1, D01 C9W8, Ireland

First published by HarperCollins*Publishers* 2025

1 3 5 7 9 10 8 6 4 2

A catalogue record of this book is
available from the British Library

HB ISBN 978-0-00-874337-6
TPB ISBN 978-0-00-874338-3

Printed and bound in the UK using 100%
renewable electricity at CPI Group (UK) Ltd

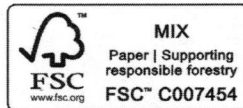

MIX
Paper | Supporting
responsible forestry
FSC
www.fsc.org
FSC™ C007454

There are so many people I would like to dedicate this book to, which is a very lucky position to be in. Three of those people have changed my life in the best way possible.

To my Theodore, Gigi and Otto.

My world, this is for you. Now listen to Mama when I say please don't read this …

Contents

Irish-English Dictionary

bogger – what Dublin people call anyone not from Dublin (technically boggers are only from the Midlands)

c'mere to me – wait till I tell you

cop on – get a grip

craic – fun

cray – crazy

deadly – brilliant

deranged – drunk out of your mind

devo – devastated

dope – idiot

Fionnuala – girl's name but also slang for vagina

gas – funny

gee – vagina

ginge – redhead

go and shite – piss off

gob – mouth

gobshite – idiot

grand – fine/good/okay

in bits – most definitely not at your best

knob – dickhead

leg it – run

loaded – rolling in it

messer – someone who fools around

minger/minging – not good-looking

press – cupboard

ride (n.) – very good-looking person

ride (v.) – to copulate with

runners – trainers

scaldy – rotten/gross

scarlation – much embarrassment

scarlet – embarrassed

scarlet for you – embarrassed for someone else

scarlet for your Ma – mortified for your mother for having you

session/'sesh' – party

shite – shit

slapper – a sexual enthusiast

sound pl. **sounders** – people that are easy to get on with

stop the lights – no way!

(to go) spare – lose it in a rage

total sounders – top shelf sounders

yer man – him
yer one – her
yoke – thing, also an ecstasy tablet
you're grand – no thanks

Let's Go

Big Mouth is the perfect name for my book. As much as I would like to be known for my amazing brain, I believe I am truly known for the size of my gob. I also love all things that are done orally – eating, talking and a few other bits I would rather keep private. Ah fuck it, I'll tell you: I enjoy catching food that people throw at my mouth because it's as big as a goal and they never miss. My mouth is my medium and I'd be lost without it and all it does for me, but it has often gotten me into trouble (mainly during my school days). Back then it was a mammoth task to try to get me to shut up; thinking back, I must have really pissed my teachers off. I know I would have found me annoying back in the day.

When I try to explain to people what this book is about, I find myself too embarrassed to say 'autobiography' because I don't feel like it is that kind of a book. To me it's a collection of stories – a lot of which include me! In general I don't read a lot of autobiographies; the only ones I read are usually written by comedians. The honesty that spills out of them is amazing and they're funny, which I like in a book. I've tried to do that here: be very honest, poke some fun at myself and go off on a few tangents. I'm like that in real life so why not in a book?

Nobody's more shocked than me that I am sitting here writing a collection of stories from my life. There's a lot of things I hope to achieve, but up till now I'd never considered writing a book with me as the central character because I don't know how much more of me people can take. While I don't have the nerve to think anyone would give a shite about what I have to say, at the same time I did want to write a book that would make people laugh, teach them a little more about me (if they're interested) and share some of the few things I've learned from life. Like everyone else I make mistakes – lots of them – and I like to repeat those mistakes over and over again, until at some point I start to understand and maybe learn a little from them. Mistakes are a very important part of life: we all make them so we need to embrace them and never be ashamed of them. (Well, maybe still a bit ashamed in private – it all depends on how shocking your fuck-up was.)

Some people think they know a lot about me from social media, but you only really get a little part of what somebody is like from their socials as it's what they choose to put up, it's a part of their lives that's curated. For instance, I don't like to show anything negative, particularly when it comes to my kids. I don't want to put anything up online that might embarrass them, like them throwing a wobbler, because it's not fair. Also, my life is too loud for Instagram – if you came to my house you would probably leave pretty quickly. For me Instagram is a mixture of fun and work and although it lands more on the side of work these days, it's a great place to be able to create good content.

Social media wasn't around when I was growing up, for which I'm forever grateful because my mother couldn't have handled the amount of cancellations that would have come my way. There tends to be hatred towards posting ad content on Instagram, but at the end of the day people have every right to make a living off it – it's their job. I hold no ill will towards them because I am one of them. I remember when I hit ten thousand Instagram followers thinking, *This is insane*. The whole thing is so odd when you think about it: wanting to see what people are doing and then endlessly comparing ourselves to them, aspiring to these distorted realities.

While my Instagram feed is full of all the fun things that I do, in reality I am a part of the dull club, the club for people who find being interesting a burden. I read an article about this and it really resonated with me because

I think my idea of fun is very different to other people's. In fact, my life could be classed as boring, which suits me fine. You might assume from the content I share on my Instagram that I live a very busy, interesting life – which at times I do – but mostly it's very chilled and family-oriented. This is where I feel at my most comfortable. That's not to say my life is completely normal. I think we're all a little bit (or a lot) weird but spend most of our time trying to put the crazy on ice and hide the mad thoughts that constantly run through our minds. (Well, that's what I do anyway.)

In this book I intend to defrost my crazy quite a bit. After reading all about it you might well end up thinking you're a lot more normal than I am. It's rare that you will ever catch me doing just one thing (I'm even eating grapes as I write this) because I'm incapable of focusing on a single task. I try to make a real effort when I am out and about to not always have something in my ears. When I was in New York doing a podcast show I forced myself to leave my AirPods at the hotel because a) I didn't want to be hit by traffic and b) I wanted to be able to enjoy my surroundings instead of hearing Dr Dre rapping about his nuts. I would love to spend a bit of time in someone else's brain because I do think mine is a little bit broken. There's always something pretty wild going on in there.

My brain is non-stop. It just doesn't have the ability to stop for a single second and I don't know if that's a good thing or a bad thing. I often wonder what happens in my brain at night when I'm asleep, some rave no doubt, somewhere like Berghain, an enormous club in the middle of nowhere in Berlin. It opens on a Friday morning and closes on a Monday. The queue is almost two hours long and it's still the place to be for very intense ravers.

Back in the day I fancied myself as a bit of a raver for a brief moment and decided I had to go. After queuing for over an hour, half of our group didn't get in and then we were faced with people who had been partying for days with no sleep. Yes, people do drugs, it's part of the rave scene, but these people DID DRUGS, and I found the experience, overall, pretty scary. I don't trust people who are so out of their mind they don't know what's going on. They probably can't trust themselves either if they haven't slept for forty-eight hours. I'm not trying to sound like I have been so sheltered that I've never been around people on drugs – believe me I have – but the intensity of this place was something else. A man started a fight with me on the way to the toilet – he said he was going to stab me and I was inclined to believe him, so we left. Apparently, I got in the way of his dancing, and he did not like that. I've heard so many rumours about Berghain, like the man who used to lie in the men's urinal waiting for men to piss on him. (I never witnessed this myself, but a sight like that might have made the trip worthwhile.) Essentially, all of this is to say, I think my brain is similar to the wild ways of Berghain.

And there's the first tangent!

Although my life is not as private as other people's, some things will always remain private. I will, however, probably divulge things in this book that I may never have done if I hadn't written it. Some of the things that have happened to me – particularly in relationships – have been awful, truly heartbreaking times, but I'll be careful not to name names. I don't do cheap shots and it's nice to have a little riddle anyway, figure out who is who. I will admit, though, that I do love reading books where people are willing to throw each other under the bus, but in the grand scheme of things, it is a bit mean. Trust me, there definitely are some people I would like to throw under a bus, use their dishonest behaviour against them, but I can't do it because I prefer to live my life drama-free as much as possible, and naming names would bring a lot of drama my way.

What really surprised me about writing this book is how much I enjoyed it. When I write I feel as though I go into my own little world where very little distracts me. It's the only time (besides when I'm sleeping) that my phone isn't even a thought in my head. It's as if I'm in a weird trance when I write; it's the closest thing I can get to meditating.

Every word in this book has been written by me. From the beginning I knew I wanted the book to be totally in my voice and to put everything I felt was needed within its pages. I want this to be a 'know what you're going to get' kind of book. You shouldn't need to call the consumer rights bureau or wherever the complaints go because it should do exactly what it says on the tin. As I am the tin, writing every word you read was imperative. I want the pages to sound like I'm talking to you, and like I've put my heart, soul, blood, sweat (actually … no, gross, cross that off) and tears into it. Some of the writing process was quite heavy so I had to take little breaks from reliving my old life, but even the hard chapters felt like a learning process. (It slightly feels like I'm verging on eulogy grounds here …)

My God. I just got a hideous pang of guilt thinking of the one eulogy I've had to give in my lifetime – my dad's. (My family is of huge importance to me and their impact will be very visible in this book.) My sister Amber and I had written half a eulogy each for his funeral and were sitting in the church front row. When the priest called our names to go up to the altar, Amber just kept repeating 'No, no, no' – that little bitch wouldn't go up and I had to read the eulogy on my own, which really threw me. I hope I did a better job than I think I did and, if not, that Dad was far too busy having fun in heaven to be looking down on us for that bit. A few nights later Amber wrote a poem about him and posted it on Facebook, definitely inebriated. It went like this:

Today is today.
Tomorrow is tomorrow.
But that won't mildly mask my tears.

When I read this I was also quite drunk and nearly choked on my Vodka Red Bull, I was laughing so much – I knew Amber would be scarlet the next day. Every year on my dad's anniversary it still comes up on Facebook and we have a great laugh about it. No offence, Amber, but I hope I make a better stab at writing this. Okay. Here we go. Thanks for joining me on the ride.

Chapter One

Look At Me

While I like pretending I only grew up in Howth, County Dublin, I did spend the first seven years of my life in Portmarnock and then Sutton (both VERY near Howth). Once I moved to Howth, though, that was it for me; I've never left it for too long and it's still where I call home. It's an unusual loyalty towards a place that some people (my husband Spencer) might not be as enthralled with as I am. How can I explain Howth to you and do her justice? First and foremost she is a peninsula who clings very lightly to Dublin because, actually, she wouldn't mind being on her own. To reach her you drive through Sutton and I'm sorry to all the Sutton Buttons out there, but sure you know yourself, you're not a patch on Mrs H!

If you don't believe me that Howth is gorgeous, I'll have to take you out for a spin and show you around properly. Now, when we drive into Howth, please let me apologise for the eyesore of apartments against the skyline (total shocker) – how they got planning we will never know, but there's not much we can do about that now. Once we drive by them, we'll reach three gorgeous piers. We might run all three of them, or walk, whatever takes your fancy. It's around 5k (the perfect distance), starting from the east pier, down the middle pier and ending on the third pier, where we can have a prawn curry at one of my favourite restaurants. Sammy the seal, one of Howth's most famous residents, will definitely be waiting for us up at his spot, bobbing away in the water. If the weather was better Howth would be the most magnificent place in the world, but even when the weather is appalling I still feel at my most relaxed there.

The best thing about Howth – besides the people – are the cliff walks; you can walk for hours just staring out at the sea. There's a great spot to go swimming and a couple of spots where you can jump from a height into the sea. We used to spend summers at the jumps, doing backflips into the water (I never backflipped but jumping was just as scary). As relaxing a place as it is, equally you will always find someone to go out with if you want to. The restaurants in Howth are stunning, the staff are sound and we have an enormous number of pubs – over twenty for our 8,000 residents. People in Howth go wild, it's in our bones – we're great craic if I do say so myself.

I love going home but I also fear it; when you go back to Howth you get sucked into the vortex. If you go for a drink in Howth, you need to be willing to commit to a twelve-hour bender and don't expect to remember too much the next day. A lot of boozing is done in Howth, but I like to think we've all matured since our teens, when we drank as often as we could get our hands on a drink (which wasn't as often as it sounds). A lot of planning had to go into a day like that, but it all felt worth it and sure, what else would we have been doing with ourselves?

Both my parents are from north County Dublin. My mom, Sandra, grew up in Sutton, although if you met her and her sisters you would think the family were from the deepest parts of County Cork with their accents. Maybe that's why I love Cork so much, because I grew up thinking my mom and aunties were from there and only pretending to be from Dublin so nobody would call them boggers. My mom has always been glamorous, chic and ladylike, a very well turned-out woman, who I have rarely – if ever – seen in a tracksuit. The only time she was spotted in a tracksuit was when she was head to toe in *My Therapist Ghosted Me* merch.

She's such a glamorous woman that God knows where I came from. (I am aware that I probably look well turned-out, but that's for work. Left to my own devices it's leggings and jumpers and I live for 'no make-up' days.)

Neither would I describe myself as chic or ladylike – I am more of a heavy-footed, loud girl. When we were kids my mom worked for Aer Lingus, which was the most glamorous job ever. She really enjoyed working as an air hostess and made great friends for life there.

My dad, Freddie, was from Skerries, another seaside town. He loved visiting the pubs and restaurants there whenever he could and being around his family. Freddie was the life and soul of the party and loved music; he always had something playing in the house or the car. Apparently, he was very attractive when he was younger, but I still found it devastating when people said how much I looked like him. One of my dad's favourite pastimes was taking the piss out of people, but he could take as good as he gave, which is important – there's nothing worse than someone who rips into you but goes mad when you return the favour. All his life he worked as a used-car salesman, but instead of working in the family garage (Annesley Williams) he went his own way and my Uncle Jim took over the garage instead. I don't know the ins and outs of why, but I think his father was very hard on him and that growing up was more difficult for Freddie than it was for his siblings. My two aunts have hinted at this but wouldn't dive any deeper because by all accounts it might be quite upsetting to hear. Still, the nosy bitch in me would love to know – if they do ever tell me, I'll be all ears and then cry my eyes out.

My dad had been married before my parents met, but it was very short, as in they-got-off-the-plane-from-their-honeymoon-and-had-it-annulled kinda short. At that time divorce wasn't available in Ireland so in a sense they were very lucky they could get it annulled and go their separate ways. I don't know what happened for it to be such a short marriage; I doubt it was good, but as far as I know it wasn't just down to my dad. They had a daughter, who is my half-sister. She's a lovely girl, but we aren't close; I did spend some time with her growing up but not too much.

Can you imagine my mother arriving home from the hospital in 1985 and introducing her new baby Vogue? It's an insane name, tacky if you will. Great for a magazine or a song but it doesn't work on a person, at least not in my opinion. Imagine when I'm a granny sitting reading my filthy sex novels and eating cake, being introduced to people as Granny Vogue? It'll be strange enough. Another annoying thing about my name is that it's impossible to take a nickname from Vogue, which bothers me. I'm now affectionately known as 'Voguey' by my friends and family, but that's a bit shite and lazy for a nickname, isn't it? When I was very young I wasn't bothered by my name although even at five years old I could see people's faces scrunch up when I said it. By the age of twelve everyone felt it was time to start slagging it and then

I started to hate my name and feel embarrassed by it. It didn't help that everyone thought I had made it up myself. As if. If I was going to make up my name, I would have gone for something like Romy or Gigi or Tiger. Sailor and River used to be on the list too ... hmmm ... I guess Vogue suits me after all! I've only ever met two other Vogues in my life and it's so nice when that happens, although one of them was a little bold so I didn't warm to her. Too like me as a child, I thought.

When I came along, baby number three, my parents already had Frederick and Amber, who were four and two years old. As kids, Frederick and I had a love–hate relationship; everyone called him 'Fred' but I wasn't allowed to and I'm still not. At this stage it feels weird calling him Frederick when no one else does (sometimes I get away with Rico). Rico calls me Fogue because he has a slight lisp and can't quite handle the V. From day one my sister Amber was and is my very best friend; she is the friend I've known the longest and I would do anything for her, as she would me. Some people (Spencer) say you can't have a sibling as a best friend, but this is my book and I say you can, particularly if you get one as good as Ambi. (The only reason Spencer claims a sibling can't be a best friend is because he likes me to say he's my best friend. He is *one* of them, but while there's nothing Amber could do to lose her best friend status, there's quite a lot Spenno could do to lose his.)

Because there are so few photos of me growing up, for a long time I was convinced I was the forgotten child of the family, but recently my mom whacked a load over to me, so I did exist. Then, when my daughter Gigi was born, I asked my mom what I was like as a child and she said, 'How would I know?' Okay. Think I remember you being there, Sandy, but whatevs! She thought I had completely lost my mind when I asked her what time I was born – which I thought was really shitty of her – but guess who can't remember what time their children were born? ME! My mom worked and did as much as she could for us, but I do think there are more expectations of mothers than there are of fathers. For instance, I expect my mother to know every last detail of my upbringing, even though she was working hard to provide and look after us. One time I asked her if she ever experienced mom guilt and she replied: 'Why would I?' How I wish I had that great attitude.

You're going to have to hear me out now because I know you'll call bullshit, but when I was very young I used to be quite shy and hated being in photos. My dad was always taking pictures of us, but I'd hide behind his leg crying and not wanting to get in. It wasn't until about the age of five that I became a massive attention-seeker; now I even smile at the speed cameras, can't get enough. It possibly had something to do with events going on in my life at that time (my parents were separating), but it certainly wasn't because I was lacking attention at home. Being the youngest I could do no wrong in my dad's eyes and I had him wrapped around my little finger. I was his favourite but, you know, I was a sound kid, so what can I say? My siblings know I was his favourite, so it won't be a surprise to them to read it here. Everyone thinks it's an awful thing to say you have a favourite child, but I completely disagree. I love all of my children deeply, but I will always favour one on any given day and it goes back and forth depending on their behaviour and I think it was the same with my parents.

My attention-seeking started out innocently enough. I'd put plasters on my forehead and cycle around our area waiting for people to ask what had happened. Then it got pretty hardcore. One time I completely faked a sprained ankle, got crutches and everything. I'd limp around on them and then leg it up the stairs when nobody was watching. Essentially, I Munchausen syndrome-ed myself for attention, but then it backfired … badly. Pretending to use an old chair frame as a kind of Zimmer frame for another leg injury I didn't have, I tried to go up a step in the shed when the bar of the chair hit me in the mouth, knocking out eight of my teeth: the four front top and bottom teeth. My whole mouth was black and blue and I had inflamed gums for so long that everyone sang 'All I Want for Christmas Is My Two Front Teeth' to me while I'd be raging and thinking, 'And all I want is for you to shut the fuck up!'

By the time I came along, I think my mom was fed up with my dad and I'd say a bit fed up with us kids too. When I was a newborn my dad took me to the pub with the intention of showing me off – Frederick and Amber were probably out playing with the traffic on that particular day. He wandered off into the pub, leaving me outside in my buggy. As luck would have it my mother was driving by (her flight was cancelled so she had the day off work) and spotted me – FURIOUS. Instead of confronting him she took me and left the buggy empty. I don't think that was a great day for old Freddie. Imagine having to go home and tell your partner you lost the baby?

I never like to call my dad an alcoholic because he wasn't someone who woke up and started drinking, but he certainly drank to excess and never had a day off. I find the word 'alcoholic' a bit aggressive and 'fond of the drink' a nicer term, so let's stick with that. My dad was fond of the drink. I would like to say here that I love my dad and always will, but I would not have wanted to be married to him. There's not much of my parents being together that I remember other than a couple of fights. Once when they were fighting I made them toast on a tray with a candle, thinking it would resolve everything.

When they separated in the early nineties, there was still no divorce in Ireland – and wouldn't be for another seven years. We had two referendums to try and introduce divorce and just over half the country voted against it the first time round. Can you imagine if we hadn't had a second referendum? Oh, how different life would be now. Imagine being forced to stay married to someone. People are crazy. I cannot imagine a world where I would choose to tell someone how to live their life – I'm too busy living my own. Imagine all the happily married people sitting on their pedestals of joy telling the rest of us to knuckle down and put up with it? It's pretty wild to think that I could have been legally forced to stay with my ex-husband.

We had to live in our house with my mom for a few weeks, then with my dad for a few weeks and then it was up to the judge to decide who we should live with full time. At that time there was a lot of prejudice against marital breakdown in Ireland, from a legal and a social standpoint, and during the court proceedings someone said that Amber and I had been eating cold beans out of a tin at our dad's house because he wasn't feeding us properly, which was total bullshit. I already had a grudge against this person, so it was hard to manage my anger! It still really pisses me off and I've hated nosy, interfering neighbours ever since. And then one Sunday at mass the priest voiced his opinions on divorces and second marriages; his opinions were less than kind so my mother stood up and told us we were leaving. When we got outside she gave us the choice to go back in, but the thrill of never having to listen to a priest go on about things

I had very little interest in was the best news ever. Maybe divorce was in fact a wonderful thing!

Even though I loved my dad, I didn't want to live with him. I knew my mother did most of the work looking after us; sure, he was the fun one who always showed up for us, but the practical side of things was down to my mom. Children like routine – it makes them feel secure and my mom ensured that we had that. My dad wouldn't have been able to have us so I have no idea why he was pushing for that to happen, more than likely it was to piss my mother off. Our dad loved us but knowing that the best place for us was with our mom he shouldn't have fought so hard. Eventually the judge said that it couldn't go to court any more, so you can imagine how many times my mom had had to endure court. I could cry writing that, I find it so sad to think of my mom going through that while looking after us three.

When we were with Dad, we spent a lot of time in the pub. He had a huge number of friends – some I liked very much, others were complete, immature assholes. They would speak to myself and Amber as if we were adults rather than very young children, and slag people off who we were close to, which is not great when you're five years of age. I remember feeling quite confused when they would say things about my mom that I didn't like, thinking they were being funny. To get them back I'd go around pouring their drinks out when they weren't looking. That was a trick I would use on my dad too. My dad would always say 'this is my last drink', but it never was. When it got to the third of his 'last drinks', I would start getting rid of it.

By comparison my kids live the greatest existence a child could have: tennis, gymnastics, swimming and park walks fill up our weekends. I won't be throwing my kids in the boot of the car and driving them to the pub while I hotbox them by smoking Benson & Hedges like our dad did. But look, they were different times back then and we did have an OK time in the pub, but there was no Monkey Music or soft play parties for us. We would play games and collect beer mats and any time he took us to the pub in Skerries we'd spend a fortune at the local carnival. Dad would give us money for the shop too, where I would purchase yet another doll and a sack full of sweets. Since then I've never been much of a pub person, and I think it stems from already having spent so much time in them as a kid. It's a 'been there done that' kind of thing.

Although it was considered new and unusual at the time, I never felt embarrassed by my parents' separation or felt like the odd one out at school. Most importantly, I never felt like I wanted my parents to get back together; even my very young mind understood they were better apart. That said, I still feel sad when I think about my parents' divorce – not for me, but for them. It wasn't the break-up of their marriage itself, but the complications involved in raising children in two different homes. The legal side of the situation was a major nightmare and my mom deserves a medal for the way she navigated her way through it. There is animosity in many families and mine is no different, but it makes me so incredibly sad. I hate it. My dad always loved my mom and I would say he regretted the marriage falling apart. Even years later he would ask me to bring pictures of her over to his house so he could see what she looked like, but the feeling was not mutual. My dad did not treat my mom the way she deserved to be treated and she has despised him ever since. I wasn't allowed to mention him at home, such was her hatred for him. It certainly made things a lot harder for us growing up, but I can understand it. It must be incredibly hard to have someone that you really dislike in your life for ever.

Chapter Two

Rich Bitch

My mom was now single and a complete ride so I would imagine she was out having a great time, although my dad and she still went to the same pub to socialise, which must have been awkward. As well as looking after us, she worked two jobs – I admire her so much for this. We didn't have much money, but I always felt like I had everything I wanted, only occasionally being turned down for a pair of Nike runners (if my brother Frederick had them, I wanted them too). My mother is such a strong person and I will always associate her with strength because she just figured stuff out, got through it and left us pretty untarnished.

We always had au pairs helping to look after us (an au pair is someone who lives with a family and works for them as well as having their own free time). The first au pair I remember was Katia. She was from Costa Rica and we really liked her. She was also a babe – even today I can remember her face – but she met a man in Ireland, married him and ditched us. She sent us her sister Majella, who was much stricter and let us get away with NOTHING, although we tried to get away with as much as we could. I would refuse to eat my cereal if it went the slightest bit soggy, but Majella would make me sit there until the bowl was empty. Whenever we wanted to have sleepovers she would barter with us: if we went and bought her a white Magnum she would let us have our friends over. Touché, Majella, touché. Strangely enough, now I actually wait for my cereal to go soggy before I eat it.

In Majella's defence I can confirm that we were difficult (to say the least), always up to something, very feral and uncontrollable – traits we still possess today. One evening it was lashing rain and the church car park had flooded, which meant it was the perfect time for Amber and me to go swimming in all of our clothes. We loved doing things like that. On that particular occasion a group of slightly older local boys started throwing coins at us, to try and hurt us I assume. We didn't care and just went around picking them up. Feral. Always on the make. Poor Majella really had her hands full with us two brats.

As kids Amber and I adored each other, but we battered each other as well, properly kicking the crap out of each other. Sometimes I would grab Amber's legs and stamp on her vagina, which probably was going a little bit too far.

I'll never ever forget one year when Amber was having a birthday party and I was jealous – because how dare the attention not be on me? She was enjoying her party, as was her right, but I was so jealous I picked up a plank of wood in the garden and whacked her across the face with it. Mom stormed out of the kitchen, pulled down my pants and slapped me on the arse in front of everyone. I never hit Amber with a plank of wood again (still kicked her in the gee though). I have to be honest, Amber and I would be partial to the odd dig even now. It usually involves a few drinks and it is always Amber's fault. I am an absolute giant and will batter her if she pushes it too far. (I would obviously never do that, but she does enjoy some rugby tackles with a few drinks on her and I just need to remind her that though she might be the boss, I am stronger!)

Every memory of my childhood involves Amber and how insane we were. I don't know if everyone was as mad as us growing up. For instance, one of us (not me) was obsessed with having a pink willy and would always go to the shop and ask the local shopkeeper Tony if he would sell us one. Unfortunately, he never had any in stock. We also used to pick up cigarette butts and smoke them, eventually graduating to stealing Dad's cigs instead. Nothing like smoking a Major cigarette when you're eight years old. If there was something we were told not to do, chances are we were going to do it. The most repulsive thing we did was pick chewing gum off the ground and eat it. I should probably take the hit for that one because I don't remember Amber telling me to do it. The chewing gum would be mashed into the ground so I would need a ruler to get it up and then I'd eat it and the little rock that always seemed to be stuck in it. The thought of it makes me feel so sick – these days I can't even share a drink with someone and there I was eating gum someone had spat out onto the street!

Amber and I did everything together and we still do. As kids we would write down our agenda for the day (we were very organised and we haven't changed). It would go something like this:

Wake up
Eat coco pops
Play shop
Swim in the swamp
Play mommies and daddies

That's a very busy day for an eight-year-old. The swamp was a weird fascination we had. I've seen it since and it's more like a giant pond, but it was one of our favourite places to go for a long time. We knew if we were caught swimming in the swamp we'd get into huge trouble. As always, we had a cunning plan. Our pals down the road had the run of their house so we'd drop in and borrow their clothes for our swamp swim and go back home in our own dry clothes, no one the wiser.

With all our activities Amber was always in charge, but I was very happy to go along with that. She would create songs and shows – she would be the songwriter and the director and I would be the performer – so I guess I kind of owe my career to her. One of her classic hits went like this: *Good morning boys and girls, good morning audience, good morning everybody in this lovely town.* My personal favourite of her songs was about her new Etonic runners (no idea where that brand went), but My God Amber Loved Those Runners. *There are a lot of runners in the world but most of all I like Etonic, Etonic.* (Repeat a million times.) Total banger.

A talented gal, my Ambi.

Amber had a very specific idea of fashion back in the day and I thought she was pretty cool. Now she has a uniform she follows; I have never seen such a large collection of shirts in my life. Sometimes I will find things I love in her wardrobe because they have been stolen off me. I am always unsure whether to mention it because I do give a huge amount of clothes away and then forget that's what I've done so it could have been a discarded item – many arguments over clothes have been started this way. We could be very charitable children at times too. One year Amber decided (it was always up to Ambi) that we should go carol-singing to raise money for charity. We got a group of pals together and went screaming around the estate with a bucket; some people gave us money pretty quickly, most likely to get rid of us. One neighbour refused to give us a penny because she thought we were keeping it for ourselves, what a witch. At that age I hadn't even considered stealing … that came to me much later.

Sometimes people would come to our doors looking for clothes, money and food and I ALWAYS gave them loads of stuff. My mom caught me one time after I'd given away my school uniform so she made me go and ask for it back. See? I'm always taking pressies back. There were a lot of toy sales going on outside our house too, organised by us, of course. We lived by the traffic lights so took advantage of the cars stopping. We'd line up all the toys we wanted to sell and some we didn't. I loved my dog Scamp who barked when you pushed him along on the stick he was attached to, but Amber got a good price for him so off he went. I was devastated. (I still am. So much so that I just googled him there and he's up for grabs on eBay for £45 quid. Buying him back is the only way I'll ever get closure from that childhood trauma.) We were always hustling in a way, it was a means to an end – the end being the shop so we could buy more sweets. I still eat sweets as often as possible; no idea how I have any teeth left in my head, especially as I like all the really bad sweets like Dip Dabs, Stinger bars, Flumps … the list goes on and on. (One of the reasons I love the colours on this book is because they remind me of a Flump.)

The first primary school I went to when I was four years old was St Marnock's in Portmarnock. We lived two houses up from it and the gates would open at 8.20 a.m., but because I'm such a freak about being on time, even when I was very little, I would turn up at the school gates at 8 a.m. So I'd stand outside in the cold just to avoid being late. In class I'd then spend a lot of time looking into the corner because I was always in trouble. Primary school is where my love of Flumps comes from: if you were good you'd get a penny marshmallow and I would just lick it until it disappeared, trying to make it last as long as possible. When we moved to Sutton I went to the Burrow School and because I was quite good at sports by this stage, I usually won the sports race. It was me against this girl Kim – I always came first but she was right there at my heels. Even though I spent quite a lot of time in the principal's office, I really enjoyed primary school.

We didn't go away very much: photographic evidence points to two holidays. Mostly we spent our summer holidays on the nearby beaches. I swear the summers in Ireland used to be better because I can remember us all walking down the road to the beach for the day. During the summer holidays the adults were like: 'Off you go, we'll see you again in September.' We had such a great time playing on the beach and just doing all the normal things that kids can't really do today for fear that someone will throw them into a white van. Nobody bothered with us brats – they'd be trying to get us out of their vans. We'd just hang out on our own and it felt safe.

We spent a huge amount of time with my Aunty Sharon, Dad's sister. He adored her although he did like to slag off her cooking. (I can vouch for her cooking, and it's delicious!) She lives in Skerries and we'd go to her for big Sunday lunches. She'd keep us all weekend with her own four kids; three sets of bunks beds and we were golden. I was scared of Sharon, but it was that nice level of I'm-your-aunt-don't-fuck-with-me scared and it still gets me today. If Sharon asked me to do the washing-up in return for a hair scrunchie I'm sure I would still jump at the chance. My nickname for Sharon is 'Triple Wick Sharon' because she loves an expensive candle and always has one lit. (When Dad died she had Jo Malone Pomegranate Noir candles lit all over the place at his wake. Now, whenever I smell that perfume I just think 'Dead Dad, Dead Dad, Dead Dad'. I once got gifted a bottle of it and because I didn't want to waste it, I forced myself to wear it but it felt like I was being swallowed by death.)

My cousin Cillian, Aunty Sharon's son, is gas. He was a total nightmare of a kid, so everyone was drawn to him, and he was my dad's favourite. Cillian knows everyone and everyone loves him. We spend a good amount of time together now and I always make sure to tell people we meet that he fancied me when we were younger because he really hates that. (It's not true but I'd never let the truth get in the way of a good story.) Cillian is what my dad would call a good time Charlie; he lives a very fun sociable life and if you're out with him don't even bother suggesting you're not drinking because he will order you a cocktail regardless. In total I have twenty-four first cousins and I'm still close with a lot of them, not because they are my cousins, but because they're sound too. Every Christmas we have a cousins lunch so we can see the cousins we don't see as often as we would like.

My mom met Neil Wilson when she was working in a restaurant and he left a big tip; Mom took the tip and pooled it with the rest of the team, which was the done thing in the restaurant. Neil was friends with my Uncle John, my mom's brother, so they must have crossed paths before, but it was only after this encounter that they started dating. At this time Neil wasn't massively wealthy (that came later) but he was doing well. The first time I remember meeting Neil was at one of Mum's dinner parties – she's a very good hostess and used to love entertaining. On that particular occasion, I had a vomiting bug and was upstairs in my bed (besides allowing me to stay in her bed and giving me boiled 7up for my tummy, my mother would not be the most sympathetic to anyone who is sick). When Neil walked in the front door, I was peering down the stairs and asked out loud 'Is that my grandad?' on account of his bald head. Say what you see and all that!

When we first met Neil we all lived in a relatively normal three-bedroom house in Portmarnock. We then moved into a house in Sutton and, as Neil's business interests progressed, into another larger house in Sutton. Then, just before my brother Alexander (Alzo) was born, Neil went from doing well to doing very, very well and all of a sudden we moved into this enormous house that sat on the cliffs of Howth with two swimming pools and a tennis court. Please don't hate me after reading that. Going from not having that much to having all of that was weird and brilliant but a bit embarrassing too. Even today, I still feel strange discussing it because it feels like we had too much. That house was ridiculously over the top, but I don't think we were spoiled; besides the house, we were treated the same as all of my other friends – just with some nice holidays thrown in.

I was CONVINCED the house was haunted and I was permanently frightened in it, mostly for dramatic effect. (Attention-seeker? Me?) When we first moved into it there was a room full of train sets, underground tunnels and a staircase that split into two. Real serial killer vibes. When my pals came over they asked me what I would do if I saw a man with an axe on one side of the stairs and

I was on the other. Do you think anything else went through my mind when I was at home alone after that comment? On top of all that, Alexander would have night terrors and walk around screaming and pointing at people that weren't there, which really didn't help matters. Two of my friends said they saw the ghost of a boy in my bedroom and the two Dobermann dogs we had used to regularly bark at nothing. That house for sure gave me a few nervous breakdowns.

Having the two swimming pools was a huge novelty and we spent a lot of time in them. I was allowed to go and swim in one on my own, even though it was away from the main house so I was unsupervised. In the pool I used to play a game where I tied myself up with a dressing gown cord and then threw myself in to see if I could get myself out from under the water. The idea that I might not have been able to get out and might have drowned never occurred to me. That memory still freaks me out today; I was only a kid but what an idiotic thing to do. It's possibly why I'm such an overprotective parent. I know what I was like when I was younger and I am not taking my chances with my kids so I worry more about them.

When I found out my mom was pregnant with Alzo I was totally heartbroken, wailing like a banshee at what should have been great news. Not a good look on me. Up until then I was the youngest and I wanted to remain the youngest, with all attention on me at all times. But when my mom told me I could use his old baby clothes for my dolls I was 100 per cent happy again. My mom always dressed us beautifully so my dolls got a great wardrobe out of it. (Now I love dressing my kids and dread the day they won't want to wear all the gorgeous clothes I buy them and will go around in football gear instead.) When Alexander finally arrived, I ADORED him, fully obsessed with my brand-new real-life doll. I was allowed to take him out for walks in his buggy, and my mom would even let me go to town and buy all his Santa presents in the toy shop. Until he was about four Alexander slept in my bed. In the morning he would try to sneak out of my room to wake up mom and Neil. To stop him I would put Vaseline on my bedroom door handle so that he couldn't open it and we all got a few more hours of sleep. Well, that 'we' didn't include me or Alzo, but Sandra and Neil slept on.

Neil grew up in a tenement flat in Dundee and because he never had a lot as a child he wasn't massively extravagant with us. He was very generous, but we were never given whatever we asked for, which at the time was disappointing. If we were rich all of a sudden, why on earth can't I order everything I want? It didn't work that way with Mom and Neil; any money we did have as kids was earned from babysitting or doing the multitude of chores flung our way. Having a big house comes with a label: 'rich bitch' was a term I did hear quite often, which confused me because I would think: *I'm not the rich one, it's not my money, it's my stepdad's*. It was tough because when you're in school you really don't want to be different to anyone else, but because of that house I was. As teenagers we used to go to a local disco called K2 and on the bus on the way home one evening a girl in my year started slagging me off about the house – with a few drinks on her she really let loose. At one point I thought she was going to hit me and as I'd never been hit by anyone in real life (apart from my siblings) it did scare me a bit. Let's just say she wasn't going to be invited to a pool party any time soon. (I joke – as if my parents would have let me have a pool party. That house was a prison palace!)

While technically Neil is my stepdad, I feel bad saying that, as I've known him over thirty years and he's essentially been a dad to me, although he can be quite serious. When we were kids there was a video chain called Xtravision, where we could rent films; on Fridays we'd be allowed to get a new release. One Friday night I chose *The Stepfather*, which had a picture of a bloody knife on the cover. When I handed it to Neil at the counter, I thought this was hilarious; looking back I still do. Neil did not. (It's fair to say that Frederick, Amber and I inherited our dad Freddie's sense of humour. We slag and prank each other constantly; once I had a red mark on my bum and so they've called me 'spot bot' ever since. Alzo is the most serious out of all of us and I reckon that's because he has Neil's genes.)

We couldn't go to Mom and Neil's real wedding in New York because my dad was being difficult and wouldn't let us travel, so my mom and Neil had a wedding party in the house. If I had known my dad was the reason we didn't get to go to New York, I would have gone turbo on him for making me miss out. Imagine all of the luminous American Fanta I missed out on drinking because of his selfish behaviour! Obviously, I missed out on the wedding too, but I'd have been more into the Fanta at the time for sure. At their Irish wedding party we all stole peach schnapps and got hammered and spent hours running across the pool cover to see if anyone would fall in. Health and safety wasn't a huge concern back then; those were the days where you'd be practically hanging off the back of the exhaust instead of being buckled up in a car seat. We never wore seatbelts until an ad came out on Irish TV with a Samantha Mumba song. In the ad it's the person in the backseat who doesn't wear a seatbelt who causes everyone to die. It scared the crap out of me and if I ever get in a car and someone doesn't put their seatbelt on I always say, 'But it was the one in the back who did the damage!' Seriously though, don't be a weirdo. Wear your seatbelt and if you won't wear one, do it on your own private time.

Neil and Sandra were always very strict. My pals knew first hand just how strict Neil was. If any of them phoned the house after nine at night he would be very annoyed and hang up on them. We weren't allowed out after school like the rest of our friends and at the weekend we would be set definite times to come home. Because we lived in such a nice house, Neil thought we should enjoy being there after school and on the weekends, but really, I just wanted to hang around the shops with my friends. Or sit on walls waiting for boys to walk by. We would leave the house in very few clothes in the depths of winter just to sit on a freezing-cold wall, thinking it was the best time ever. I'm surprised we all didn't get an outbreak of piles.

One time Neil was going through maths homework with me (my first mistake) when he realised I was using my calculator for some times tables (my second mistake). All hell broke loose – I had to spend the next three hours learning my times tables. I still excel at them today! I always think of him as the smartest man I know although when he was around four he and his friends did play a game of chicken with the traffic. This essentially involved being the last person to move out of the way of a moving vehicle. Obviously he wasn't too quick as a four-year-old, so ended up with two broken legs. Before he told me this story, I would have assumed that even at that age he would have been more advanced than us, but it turns out he's just as stupid as the rest of us.

We always had a long list of chores to do. Neil grew up having to do the same: 'nothing was ever handed to me on a plate' is one of his favourite expressions and he wanted to teach us the value of hard work. (He once told me a story that he kept leaving the door of the flat open and his mother got so fed up she took it off the hinges.) Do you remember the referee who hosted the original TV show *Gladiators*? Well, I always liken Neil to him. Frederick, Amber and I each had a phone in our room and Neil would conference call us at 8 a.m.: Amber hoover the stairs, Frederick wash the cars, Vogue make breakfast and clean the kitchen. He would round off the conversation like this, in his very Scottish accent.

'Amber, you will go on my first whistle, Vogue, you will go on my second whistle, Frederick on my third!!'

And we went!

What a lovely little gang of cleaners!

In his later years Neil has taken on some chores himself; he makes my mom breakfast in bed every morning and if they ever have a fight and aren't talking she'll punish him by refusing it. Oh no, Sandy, please, I really want to make you eggs! They've been married for thirty years now and have a great relationship. Neil is so lovely to Mom and while she is very nice to him, she could pick up the game in certain areas. For their most recent anniversary Neil bought her some beautiful jewellery, a very generous and thoughtful gift. Mom bought Neil six golf balls! She also let it slip that she has given him the same wash bag three years in a row and he hasn't noticed. (Shite present anyway, I can see how it's so unmemorable!)

Altogether Neil and Mom lived in that beautiful house on the cliff for fifteen years; I was heartbroken when they sold it. It went up for sale recently and I went to view it – I couldn't afford it but the estate agent thought I could so I snuck in that way. It really is a dream house but, as my mother would say, a money pit. While I was there, I thought I'd chance my arm and try to view the house next to it, also a beauty and on the market for 15 million. But by that point the estate agent had cottoned onto me so I didn't even make it up the driveway. He then had the audacity to show me places outside Howth, to the point where I thought: 'This lad has no clue what I'm looking for, he'll be showing me houseboats next.' In the end the house on the cliff was bought for a young couple by their loaded parents, the lucky bastards. Recently, Ireland's Eye, an uninhabited island just off Howth, went up for sale. The last I heard it was full of rats, but I have no real evidence of that. I fantasised about buying it because then I could be the Mayor of Howth, but when I told my pal Mego about this dream she quickly reminded me that she was and always will be Mayor of Howth.

Chapter Three

Santa Sabina and the Teenage Witch

When I started secondary school at twelve years of age, I was the same height as everyone else; then, shortly after, it was as if someone just pulled me like Stretch Armstrong. Overnight I turned into this huge green giant. I say green giant because we had a green uniform – none of my pals were particularly creative when it came to slagging anyone. I also liked sweetcorn so it did make sense, in fairness to them. My mouth was always enormous, but because I had stretched so quickly, I now looked like a stick with a massive gob, a bit like that filter on Instagram that transforms your whole face into a mouth. At the time I was obsessed with headbands, they were all I wore in my hair. (Until I started secondary school, I had never had my hair in a ponytail – my mom has had short hair her whole life so anything past a good brush was not her forte. I always swore I would learn all the French plaits and cool hairstyles for when my own daughter came along but they're very hard to master. Thankfully Gigi refuses to have anything but pigtails so it suits us all down to the ground.)

Puberty is rotten, but I found it put a lot of pressure on me, mainly because I didn't have a tit to the name. I was desperate for a bra that I didn't need, but my mom never offered to get me one because there was, as I said, no need. I still sometimes wish I had bigger boobs, but then people with bigger boobs wish they had smaller ones so I guess we all want what we don't have. When I got measured recently, I put my bra size on my Instagram bio – they told me I was a 30D, which isn't a big size, but people assumed I was bullshitting and couldn't possibly be as big as a D cup. It really bothered some people but I'm taking it and am beyond thrilled. When I'm out for the night I have my special going-out bras with triple padding; my boobs look enormous in them and if for any reason I was to be punched in the tit (entirely possible in my friendship group) I wouldn't feel a thing.

My period came late so I spent a lot of time praying to the period gods for it just to happen – at sixteen my wish came true. It was the first and last time I enjoyed a period, except for those few times in my adult life where it has arrived late, nearly giving me heart failure. The day I finally got my period I changed my pad about twenty times, each time telling everyone I was off to change my pad AGAIN because now I was Queen of the Heavy Flow. It wasn't until I recorded a podcast on puberty with a couple of doctors, who explained it all to me, that I realised it is quite fascinating. We all know that during puberty there are hormones flying around everywhere, but something that really stuck in my mind from that conversation was that whatever you teach yourself during puberty will stay with you for life. How I wish mine had been something other than song lyrics and rap battles. I would buy albums, take out the paper sleeve and listen to the song while learning the lyrics at the same time. I can still remember the entire rap to Outkast's 'B.O.B' and that is a fast rap track, my friends. I have made some use of it and break it out almost every time I drink, swiftly followed by video footage of me giving birth, which I should just delete from my phone because it's getting embarrassing how many people have now witnessed that private and special moment!

I went to Santa Sabina, which is an all-girls school that was down the road from my house. In Ireland you go to the school that's closest to your house, unless your parents have notions and send you off to the fee-paying schools. No offence to any of the fee-paying families, but I do believe the Irish schooling system is above average, so why bother spending that money if you don't have to? How hypocritical you may say – and you would be dead right because my kids go to a fee-paying school in

London, but that's only because I was told I had to do that and you'll learn from this book that I mostly believe anything I'm told. I still shudder when I think of paying for schools and if I could move back to Ireland for the schools alone I would.

The system in London is mad. Spencer went into Theodore's school when he was one day old to get signed up. It seems so ridiculous – and it is – but everyone was at it. We had a friend who paid someone nine grand to sign their child up to loads of schools; they didn't even get the one they wanted in the end. I do really love T and Gigi's school so it was worth standing outside there a day after giving birth. Yep, I went along for the ride, to prove how much we wanted our brand-new baby in that school!

My mother and all her sisters also went to Santa Sabina when they were younger, and my Aunt Naomi became an art teacher at the school. In a strange turn of events she ended up teaching my Aunty Sabina (her younger sister and, yes, she was named after the school!) and Sabina did not like that at all. In all fairness, I would have hated for Amber to have any authority over me in school too. Naomi told me a story of how one time she asked Sabina's class to clear up the room and when they'd finished, Sabina stayed behind and gave out to Naomi for telling her what to do!

Naomi is my godmother and one of the nicest people in the world. For my birthdays she used to buy me goats, pigs and chickens to give to families in Africa. Essentially, she'd give me a piece of paper, which I hated at the time, but looking back it was the perfect gift. Buying her presents is tricky though, because she has an awful habit of regifting things. I reckon she has regifted everything I have ever bought her, and the reason I think this is because she once gave me something back that I had already given her! One year I thought I would outsmart her so I gave her a hairdryer with her name engraved on it. Not one to be fooled, Naomi gave it to my younger cousin, conveniently named Naomi (little Naomi and big Naomi).

Big Naomi had the misfortune of being my year head when I was in fourth year of school, which was one of my monster years as a teenager. My sister Amber and I got nicknamed 'the monsters' by my stepdad Neil because we were complete arseholes that nobody could handle, although I think most girls are to be avoided from the ages of fourteen up because my pals were much the same as me. Amber was a couple of years ahead of me in school and was very politely asked to leave because her behaviour was not in line with the school's standards – they felt she would be better suited somewhere else. (She wasn't, the new school didn't know what to do with her either.) She got caught for everything but I was much sneakier and never got caught. Well, not legally anyway; they knew what I was up to but could never prove anything.

During one bout of being grounded Amber decided the best thing to do would be to bring the fun to her. She was babysitting Alzo and invited her friend up, who kindly brought a litre of tequila with him. As they wanted to get drunk quickly they decided to start shotting it. Her friend was really tall, about six foot four, but he was still the one to fall first and started puking in the downstairs toilet. Amber then put him under her bed to try and hide him from my parents, but as her bed was a four-poster brass bed two feet off the ground you could see him perfectly. What an idiot. When my parents got home, they saw pretty quickly that Amber was deranged and then noticed the stench of vomit from the toilet. Within minutes her friend was located and Neil went straight onto his parents. He then decided to call the Rutland centre for Amber (an addiction recovery centre in Dublin). It was at that moment that Amber realised she had really messed up. The Rutland centre never materialised but Amber was barely allowed to breathe for some time after that.

I'm a rat, it's in my bones, and to this day I still tell tales on my siblings. If Amber wasn't caught that night, chances are I would have told that story anyway. She told me once she had smoked a spliff and I thought this was a slippery slope for Amber: she'd be on the streets in no time. I imagined her destitute, walking around Dublin city with no shoes on … far-fetched

I know, but my mind takes me to the most ridiculous places. It was my duty to make sure this was not her future. Genuinely worried for her, I told my parents straight away and made them say Nola the gardener had told them. Poor Amber never stood a chance, she had a rat in her midst.

In secondary school I made friends with a group of girls who are still my friends now – shout out to the Girlos. One of my best friends from this group is Ashely; we have been friends for twenty-six years, which makes me feel ancient. Our dream was always to be able to work together and as Asho is now a make-up artist, we often do – it makes me so happy. Asho is one of the nicest people in the world and someone I will be friends with for ever. Ashley cannot bear to look at the news because it worries her too much; I love the fact that World War Three could break out yet she would be none the wiser. We spent so much time together when we were younger and when I go home to Ireland we still do, but now it's with our kids who absolutely love each other. My husband thinks it's wild that I'm still so close to the girls I went to school with. He assumes people grow apart but we always stayed close. Asho would know most things about me and I can trust her with anything – that's pretty rare to have outside of family. We were each other's brides-maids and she was there for me when (surprise, surprise) my first marriage imploded. (More on that later.)

Whenever I go back to Ireland, I always make plans with Asho and my pals in advance, to make sure I get to see them. No matter how much time has passed we just pick up from where we left off and I feel very lucky for that because long distance friendships can be hard to maintain. Having people I can trust, who I don't need to keep secrets from or worry that they will pass on private information is something I'm very appreciative of. (We have just organised our girls' trip for our upcoming forti-eth birthdays. I thought we would lose a few of the Girlos, such was the annoying extent of the group chat, but after what seemed like a lifetime we managed to book somewhere!)

At school I was a frequent visitor to the principal's office. I still maintain that it was only my mouth that got me into trouble: I just couldn't stop talking, adored distracting anyone I could and sent notes incessantly. Good times. I never considered that I was stopping not only myself from learning but other people too and that the teachers didn't like that. Our principal was insanely posh and at one of our meetings she took it upon herself to teach me how to look people in the eye; we were all terrified of her and I had to sit in silence having a staring contest with her. To this day, however, I have great eye-contact skills as a result.

Looking back I can probably see other elements of my behaviour, apart from messing, that were far from reasonable. In fourth year (we call it a transition year in Ireland), you go out of school and do work experience. Mine was supposed to be doing make-up with my friend at a TV station where her mom worked, but she cancelled on us at the last minute so we just sat in her house for two weeks. We had a lovely time, loads of TV, a few naps but absolutely zero work. Overall the Girlos and I were major messers. Once in art class two of my friends were using silver metallic paint. When one of them put a small bit of the paint on the other girl, she picked up the two-litre tin and poured it all over her in retaliation (she had a very short fuse). Metallic paint doesn't wash off and should not be put on your skin and Naomi was desperately trying to get it off my friend. Later I found out that Naomi bought her a new school uniform, which again shows you how nice she really is.

Our school had a strict uniform policy, but of course I liked to bend the rules. We all went through a big phase of wearing Xworx and Nope everything and whatever we could buy in Miss Sixty, drowning ourselves in CK One or Tommy Girl. I've started wearing CK One again and the nostalgia from it is insane. It's like taking a huge sniff into your past. Perfume has a way of doing that. One time Spencer bought Cool Water, which is my stepdad Neil's exclusive perfume and I was revolted when he tried to kiss me smelling like Neil. I've met men who I've immediately disliked and then realised it was because they smelled like an ex-partner, same scent. They could be a ten out of ten but if you smell like an old flame, it ain't happening.

For most of school I was constantly washing make-up off my face in the bathrooms and we all wore pyjama bottoms under our kilts because the school was like the Antarctic. To try and avoid wearing school shoes I'd sneak in wearing runners, but eventually they outsmarted us and bought rotten-looking slippers that they made us wear when we arrived in runners. Naomi spotted me in them once and was thrilled to see I had been reprimanded; she said, 'I bet you feel stupid now' to which I replied: 'No actually, Naomi, I think they're really cool.' We were quite picky about what shoes were cool enough to wear and 'Dubes' were not on that list. 'Dubes' are sailing shoes from Dubarry and a lot of kids over the posh side of the city, the Southsiders, wore them. Although they were not cool on the north side, I liked them so I wore my sister's pair for one day. Never again. I had forgotten what a pack of bitches my friends were (including myself) – they slagged me all day long.

The school had a canteen where they sold plain and buttered rolls, some revolting soup, and gave you hot water for your Pot Noodle. When Spencer told me about his school lunches I couldn't believe my ears, but then he did go to Eton and if I spent that much money on my child for school I would want them dining on caviar too.

(I may bend the truth sometimes; they didn't have caviar but they did get chili con carne and so it was classy all the same.) At break we'd find an empty classroom and sit on the desks to eat our lunch; my aunt Naomi had the biggest and brightest classroom so we usually took that one for our own. If anyone had brought in anything decent to eat (chocolate was top of the list), the first of us to say BITS got to have some, unless the person with the decent lunch shouted NO BITS first, then they got to eat their lunch without having to share. It was a great system and we all followed the rules. Unless someone wanted a crisp, then you bunched them all at the end and held your hand around it so nobody could get any. One of the girl's moms used to bring her a chipper complete with curry sauce. BIIIIIIIIIIITS. Looking back it shouldn't have been allowed because none of our moms were nice enough to ever bring us something that delicious. From the age of eleven I made my own lunch, which meant I spent my lunch money at the garage by the school on a bottle of coke, three croissants, a bar of chocolate and two packets of crisps. This ritual went on until a teacher looked in my bag and told my mom I couldn't be bringing that into school any more. Considering I then largely survived on Pot Noodles, I've turned out fine (chicken and mushroom all the way.)

It really is amazing that you end up learning anything at school, particularly for someone like me who made it extremely difficult for themselves. School for me was about having fun and I never took learning too seriously. My mom made us all go to study after school, which meant we stayed back until 5.45 p.m., supervised by Sister Mary, who was quite nice but not to be messed with, and Sister Paul, who would eat you for lunch if you took a step wrong. I spent most of my study time writing notes to my friends who I had just spent the entire day with. My favourite of all the nuns was Sister D., a joy to the school. I often wonder whether we'll still have nuns in the future; the last time I saw a nun was when I went to see *Sister Act* in the West End. I still see a fair few priests knocking around, but nuns are definitely on the out. I know some nun orders haven't got a great reputation in Ireland but we got lucky with ours. I'm actually going to meet a couple of them soon, organised by Aunty Naomi, of course.

Studying always ramped up around exam times and I would be sent to my room to do it, but I figured out a pretty nifty napping system. I would lie on my bed and cover my face with my science book so it would look like I fell asleep because I was so exhausted from all the studying. In my defence, I am one of those people who don't believe in exams for young people; it puts far too much pressure on them and continuous assessment is much better, in my opinion (not that anyone asked for it). Before exams I would spend a long time writing notes on my legs; so long in fact, that if I'd actually just sat down and studied it would have taken less time. It was like my brain turned off when I had to study for exams because I didn't want to do it. Even in college, when I was writing a 10,000-word dissertation on wave energy that I was actually interested in, I couldn't focus because I *had* to do it. Now I'm writing 80,000 words for this book and I love it, because I don't have to do it. I've chosen to do it. Moral of the story: if you want me to do something don't make it compulsory.

Chapter Four

Dry Riding

I had my first drink when I was twelve, which was quite the transition considering I had a doll until I was eleven. It was my first year of secondary school and my new pals and I immediately planned when we would try booze. We got ourselves a litre bottle of Bulmers cider, which we shared between six of us, and decided we were hammered. Soon after that we started hanging outside our local off-licence asking strangers to go in and buy us drinks. We had no shame and a surprising amount of people were okay with buying alcohol for thirteen-year-olds, luckily for us. One weekend my friend had a free gaff so we all told our parents we were having a sleepover, omitting to tell them that her parents weren't home. We decided that we would get a bottle of tequila between each pair of us (half a bottle each) and that would do the job. It did. I don't remember too much of that night but

I do remember waking up the next morning to bodies lying everywhere. One of my friends was fast asleep with half of her body hanging outside the back sliding door, which I thought was pretty impressive.

After that particular slumber party, it was twenty-six years until I was able to drink tequila again, that hideous little monster. On the odd occasion when we couldn't get an adult to buy us booze, we would do the obvious thing and steal it from our parents. Everything – vodka, whisky, gin – would go into an empty 500ml bottle of coke, topped up with coke. Completely hideous but effective. We would drink it up on the golf course near our house and stumble around in our O'Neill's tracksuit bottoms and Buffalo shoes until we had sobered up and could go home – oh, but not before we had kissed everyone. We went out a fair bit when we were younger, mainly to teenage discos and if I was staying at my dad's we would be off to the Southside to 'Wesley', the top tier of discos and where most of the rides our age went. School got in the way a little bit but I took time off when needed, a little week suspension did me no harm. One of the best things to do (and we would always beg our parents for money for it) was to go to Winter Party. It was held in The Point Depot (known as the 3 Arena) and hosted 5,000 underage drunk teenagers with fluffy leg warmers stuck to their legs, wearing bandanas as tops. I would also wear a bandana on my head. Bandana girl!

The Winter Party was a very big event in our calendars and we loved it. Pre drinking began near the venue and then we would head in, ready to compete in one of the largest ever games of beat the slapper. You probably can't call it that now but the game was that you had to go around and kiss as many boys as you could throughout the night. Absolutely rotten. It makes my stomach turn to think about it now. Again, I can't even share a drink with somebody yet there I was going around, mouth hanging open waiting to trap anyone that came my way like a mackerel. Violent. One of my pals did so well at the game that her face broke out in cold sores not long after! It was around that time we stopped playing that hideous game.

My first kiss was deeply unmemorable (as is anyone's), so much so that I can't really remember it at all. I was about twelve and really didn't want to do it but was forced into it by my sister and her friend Lynn. I was friends with her brother and we all spent a lot of time together because our parents were friends and we all went to the same place on holidays. I knew I fancied him one day when he arrived down at the beach in Portugal. These were the days when I still only wore bikini bottoms because I didn't have boobs and there was no need for a top. I was swimming away having a great time on my body board when I spotted him and died a little bit inside. I didn't want to get out of the water with no top on because he would see me – not much to see, but I still felt incredibly embarrassed, so I stayed in the sea until everyone went up for lunch. This might have been minutes or hours – I don't actually know – but I was frozen by the time I got out.

At one of our parents' dinner parties Amber and Lynn decided that myself and her brother had to kiss. There was to be no complaining and we were sent into the toilet with the lights off and the door shut until we had done it. So there you have it, the most unromantic thing in the universe orchestrated by Amber and her pal. As we got older, I was eventually allowed to hang out with them and I stole Lynn, which Amber hated. Lynn is great fun. When we were in our late teens she got dumped by a lad she was mad about, who looked eerily similar to Jimmy Nail. To cheer her up I took her down to a festival in Ireland called Electric Picnic, but poor Lynno was devo. She'd be full of fun but then would suddenly start crying, so we would have to drink more to cheer ourselves up.

We had the misfortune of bumping into her ex, aka 'Jimmy Nail', which really made things take a turn for the worse. Personally I thought he looked like shite but Lynn was into shite at the time so was even more heartbroken. Without getting myself into too much trouble on these pages I did what any good friend would do and got slightly incoherent with her until Jimmy was barely a faint memory. We ended the night in our car (in the car park – nobody was driving, obviously) and Lynn treated us to a dance party. We put on the headlights and she danced in front of the car until we thought we would get sick laughing. All of us took a turn, naturally, and this went on for hours, the song 'Put Your Hands Up For Detroit' was on repeat.

Tangent!

As a teenager I wasn't particularly desirable, but as I've never been that attracted to good-looking men it worked out well for everyone involved. We all went through phases of fancying one of the ten boys we hung out with and at some point or another we kissed most of them. We'd swap boyfriends like there was no tomorrow, although a couple of friends would claim boys and you weren't allowed near them even if that boy had no inter-est in your pal – girl code, don't touch. I was a bit of a prude, but it wasn't because I didn't want to have sex. I was just desperately scared of everyone thinking I was a slut, which would have been awful. Looking back I shouldn't have given a shit, but that was the worst thing that someone could call you back in my teenage years.

Instead I resorted to dry riding (what a grim but perfectly descriptive word, mimicking sex while wearing all your clothes or rubbing up against each other). The problem for me was that, eventually, everyone started to move on. The boys were putting their hands up our tops and as I hadn't a tit to my name, I was petrified of that ever happening. I envisioned kissing someone I really fancied and then, when they put their hands up my top, their hands would just keep going until they reached my head. I didn't even have the suggestion of a boob and in the lying down position my chest went inwards. (That's as sexual as I'm going to get in this book because I am still a prude in many ways and diving into the hideous encounters of teenage life would require more Xanax than I could ever get my hands on.)

There have been many shameful moments in my life, but one that really stands out was when I was fourteen and my pals and I had been drinking with a group of guys we thought were so cool (way better than the boys we had been hanging out with so it was best behaviour all round). There were some miscalculations on my part with the amount of drinking I had been doing, which was a common theme. Drinks had been taken and I tried to kiss one of the really hot ones, but the humiliation didn't end there because the drunk me continued to try to kiss him regardless of how many times he turned me down. That scarlation will never leave me, there's a special place in the pit of my stomach for that one. Looking back, though, I do admire his resilience because I would have pity-kissed someone after a while. I must have been so revoltingly drunk that he couldn't bring himself to even do that. My friends made that one very difficult to forget, but I would have done the same in their position. It took quite a while for that night to fade from anyone's memory.

Those early teenage years the whole boyfriend thing was very awkward. One of my sort-of boyfriends said he would ring me after school and I nearly died because I had nothing to say to him and he wasn't exactly the biggest talker. At home I wrote down a few notes of topics we could talk about so it wouldn't be awkward. It was awkward though and soon after that the relationship came to a natural end. Another time I went out with a very good-looking boy that everyone fancied for a while; to be fair to him he is very good-looking today (and still lives down the road). I'm pretty sure he cheated on me with my pal, but again, I'm not sure and I don't think I cared too much at the time because I started going out with his pal immediately afterwards, then got bored very quickly and gave him the boot.

Getting the boot was something you had to get used to at fourteen/fifteen. It's around that age you go to the Gaeltacht (an Irish rite of passage). There are Gaeltachts in different parts of Ireland where the locals still speak Irish and in the summer they kindly open their doors to teenagers from all over the country to help them improve their Irish (which we all study at school). The main reason we're there though is to score any and every boy or girl we can. It's often the first time you get away from your parents and are left to your own devices so it's thrilling – needless to say I had a ball although one boy I kissed down there sent his pal over to dump me, what a wanker.

Writing this I can still picture his face – he was not too gorgeous himself, to be honest. Soon after I went out with his ginger pal; I have and always will have a special thing for a ginge.

All of my life there has definitely been an emphasis placed on the way people look, myself included. From an early age people would comment on my appearance, which there is nothing wrong with if you're calling a child 'cute' or whatever, but it's the only way I can pinpoint how I started noticing mine and other people's looks. I think a lot of us have appearance issues – well, I can't say all because Spencer wouldn't change a thing about himself. He laps himself up and couldn't think of a better body to have landed in. When I first met him I found this so fascinating and I still do sometimes – it's amazing to be like that. To be so happy and fulfilled with yourself must be a great thing. He also doesn't ever feel embarrassed about anything, which makes me think he might be an alien, but I've never seen him outside of his human form so I can't be 100 per cent sure. I admire his attitude to how he looks and who he is – in some ways I'm quite envious of it.

It's taken quite a bit to get to a place where I'm comfortable in my own skin and there are still (always) a few wobbles. The first time I remember feeling embarrassed of myself was when I was a teenager. Very skinny with zero boobs, I was a tall gangly thing with an enormous mouth and even bigger spade hands that I would try to hide. I looked exactly like one of the aliens from *Mars Attacks!* for many of my earlier years, and I towered above the boys. Oh, how I would have loved to have been petite with little bird-like legs instead of my football player ones. I still to this day hold my hands in a certain way in pictures and the calves on me? Well, they are still strong and it's still difficult to find the right boot. All of my pals had boobs and the boys fancied them a lot more than they fancied me. Can't blame them, I wouldn't have fancied me either.

As teenagers we all did what we could to enhance ourselves. The make-up was extraordinary, especially when you see what the teenagers are doing with themselves nowadays. We wore bright eyeshadow, orange foundation and a streak of glitter along our cheeks. We would all straighten our hair with an iron and ironing board, losing chunks of it in the process. Fake tan had just come on the market (well, in our young eyes it had anyway) and did we make use of that! The tan was crap (nothing like the Bare By Vogue Williams of today ;-)) and we would all go around with luminous orange hands. To try and remove it I used bleach. Bleach! Can you imagine? It really did work but my hands felt like sandpaper after. I'm not sure how we figured out that bleach got rid of tan, but as I was very domesticated for my age

I likely assumed if it cleaned a stainless-steel sink, I could be quite sure it was going to clean my hands. Taking the top layer of skin with it of course.

When I was sixteen, I grew into myself a bit more – my mouth seemed smaller at least – but then I started hating my body; I thought I was the fattest person in the world with the most revolting legs. To try and slim them down I'd walk around the hill of Howth … (My God I love Howth and have toyed with the idea of dedicating an entire chapter to it, but my editor is so jealous that she doesn't live there so won't have it!) While I didn't know much about exercise back then I did know that walking made you lose weight if you went fast and stuck to hills so that's what I did. As Howth is basically a collection of hills and cliffs, after school I would alternate days between the hill and the cliff walks. At 5.45 p.m. every evening, after study with Sister Mary and Sister Paul, I would go straight home then head out for my steps. Without even knowing it the calmness of those evenings on my own was probably very helpful for my mind, although the main focus for me was to work out. The cliffs, especially when tourist free (do not go near them on a weekend morning), are the most serene place in the world. All you can hear is the wind, and the smell of the sea still fills me with happiness every time. (Not down at the harbour though, that stinks.) It did become a little obsessive, but to be honest walking is still one of my favourite things to do. I imagine I will book a lot of walking holidays when my kids don't want to hang out with me any more.

To keep it interesting for myself I did a lot of people-watching on those walks and it's still one of my favourite pastimes; sometimes I want to put certain people in a box just so I can stare at them, like Brad Pitt. Not just because he's a ride but because it would be interesting to have a good gawk. I know this gives a bit of 'lotion in the basket' Hannibal Lector vibes, but I just want to look at people – I don't intend on eating them! My mom is the same. She takes it even further and has a pair of binoculars in her room so she can get a better look at people on their walks: voyeurism at its finest. When she was younger, her family lived by a beach and her sisters told me that she would spend hours by the shore, no swimming or anything, just staring people out of it.

One evening, while my friend and I were walking along minding our own business and staring at people, one of my oldest friends (a boy) drove around after us shouting things out the car window. It was quite intimidating and very rude so that was the end of him and his poxy family. Grudges are something I am very well equipped to hold, shockingly so, and that friend of mine will be someone I never talk to again. Years later he actually lived quite near me and I still ignored him; he doesn't have great vibes generally and I met a girl who used to go out with him who confirmed it and that was good enough for me. If someone annoys or is awful to me or someone I love, they will go straight onto my list of enemies. Not much goes on in that list; it's just one I have in my head reminding myself which people are no-goers. My loyalty knows no bounds and I am fiercely protective of the people I love. I do expect the same loyalty in return and for the most part I've been lucky in that sense but, every now and then, a few cockroaches do make their way in (more on that later).

One of the things my so-called friend shouted at me from the safety of his car full of his friends was not to bother walking the hills because I would always have thunder thighs. It was all the rage to have stick-thin legs, ones that you would find hanging out of a bird's nest, so I took that really badly. From then on, I became obsessed with food and how I could avoid it whenever possible. It's very hard to assert your authority when you're younger so I became quite inventive. I would make a sandwich and pack my school lunch as normal with whatever else I thought my mom would be happy with, but I just wouldn't eat it. Instead I'd fill a sandwich bag with Special K and try to survive on just that for the day. Why hadn't I thought of that before? This was the time of the Special K diet, which was a fantastic marketing tool; all it involved was eating three bowls of the stuff a day to lose weight. It all made sense to me; I hadn't really learned too much about nutrition and just thought Special K plus very little else would make me skinny. For the record, Special K is not healthy, it's ultra-processed. I wish I knew back then what I now know about food. I thought eating as little as possible was the only way to lose weight and I always felt hungry.

There is one famous Special K story in our family. One time Ashley came for a sleepover and the next morning we were making breakfast (Special K, of course). When Ashley spilled some dry cereal on the floor and went to bin it, Neil spotted her and told her to put it back in the bowl because his floor was clean! Classic Neil. Hates waste and has a short fuse. He's actually been banned from the O2 shop in Edinburgh and a bank because he threw a Nellso wobbler, whoops! Sometimes, when Alzo gets annoyed you can almost see him transform into Neil, he's like the hulk getting ready to lose it with you.

Eventually my mom noticed my new eating habits so she started the Special K diet too! (I'm joking.) I had lost a good bit of weight, had become strange around food and she was really worried and forced me to sit down and eat dinner. To my horror she wouldn't let me leave the table until I had finished. Eating dinner was the worst thing I could do – proper food like pasta and chips were everything I hated at that time. I can vividly remember coming home with a pair of Diesel jeans that I'd had to get a in a bigger waist size. The aim was to get smaller, so this meant that I was failing. If I really try to unpack it I've always been uncomfortable with my height. I would love to be five foot eight, which sounds strange to people who want to be tall, but to me, small and petite equalled feminine. Throw in a pair of stick-thin legs and that would have been my dream come true.

My weirdness with food went on for over a year, until I discovered training as a way of managing my weight. (I was always very sporty and better at that than anything academic, but of course I gave all of that up when I found boys and alcohol.) It's no secret that I love training, but now my love of it is more to do with the way it makes me feel rather than how I look. We had a small home gym, but I hadn't a clue what I was doing so I stuck to cardio machines as they were the easiest to navigate. I wasn't training properly then – reading a book on a bike is hardly going to raise the heart rate – but I did feel in a better headspace after it and that's still my main motivation for training. People are under the impression that I work out non-stop and while I'm active most days (usually five days a week), I only train for about thirty minutes at a time. I wish I still played hockey because it's really good fun; my sister played a lot but she was the goalie so that's not real hockey. She was always cold on the pitch, which would suggest she didn't move around much.

Food is one of the greatest pleasures in life and it's sad to look back and think what a young girl who doesn't like her body will deny herself, just to fit into a pair of jeans. I didn't study home economics at school because Neil told me business studies was a better class. What a load of shit. I wanted to make cakes and sew and learn about health and nutrition. I know a lot more about nutrition now than I did when I was sixteen, but I really wish I'd known it back then. Food education is so important and yet so many people still don't understand it because the information certainly isn't given to us growing up. Now I have figured out a pretty good balance with myself: I train and eat healthily but follow the 80/20 rule and I never ever diet any more. In a restaurant I will always order what I want. As I am health-obsessed I do try and ensure I'm putting the right things into my body, but I still have a big sweet tooth so chocolate is here to stay.

By seventeen I had more or less grown into my mouth and I was no longer a skinny little alien-looking thing with shovels for hands, so I got a bit more attention. I was shaking off my grey feathers and I even embraced my name; having a sprinkle more confidence meant that people suggesting it was a cringe name didn't even touch the sides with me any more. The idea that I invented my name myself does still follow me around but we must give Sandra credit where credit is due, she was adventurous with names. It's probably helped with my career in a way because when you're called Vogue more people tend to remember you. It's a difficult name to forget. My height makes me more memorable too, so put them both together and it works a treat.

Chapter Five

Wannabe

Modelling was something I was always interested in growing up but mostly because I saw it as a gateway to fame, which was a bit of an obsession for a lot of kids in the nineties and noughties. When I was eleven, I was invited to my friend's fancy dress birthday party and instead of being a normal child and dressing up as a princess, I went as a model. Now, if a child turned up to my house dressed as a model I would think, 'What a wanker', and scarlet for their parents. (I am scarlet for my parents for letting me do it!) Anyway off I went in my deep purple Miss Selfridge suit and cream Kickers shoes that I wore for my confirmation. A model I was not, more of an underage child off to work in an office.

The party was in a house in Howth and the girl's name was Julie – I can vividly remember what she looked like; her hair was thick and luscious (mine has always been of the thin variety). It was your average kids' party except her house was massive (this was before we had upgraded ourselves) and I remember being in awe that someone would live somewhere so fancy. I still miss all the games we used to play at those parties like pass the parcel and musical chairs, where inevitably someone would end up with a nosebleed as it became increasingly competitive. I was a lingerer, that was my technique: eye up a chair and make it mine. Shite toys were my forte and I wanted to go home with that slinky, nosebleed or not.

My first peep at the entertainment industry was in the halls of Santa Sabina. A TV company came by to shoot an ad there for Bank of Ireland or something and a few of us got selected to stand in the hall as extras. It was our big moment and we loved every single dull moment of it. When the ad came out we were all blurred and there was only the merest suggestion of us – you couldn't even see our faces. Scarlet for us because we had told anyone who would listen about it and you could barely see us. We were not stars!

Oh no, I have just unlocked a memory that was so embarrassing I must have pretended it didn't happen, such was my quest to work in TV. I went on a modelling course, can you fucking imagine? A MODELLING COURSE! My parents clearly wanted me out of the house if they were willing to pay for me to go to someone who taught me how to walk, talk and sit straight. It feels kind of medieval now that I think about it, more finishing school than modelling school. I don't remember any of us on the course being model worthy or even particularly good-looking at our awkward teenager stage – we were a class full of minging models, myself included.

In the fifth and sixth years of school I went through my girl-band era. I would audition to be in different girl-bands and sometimes get pretty far in the audition process, but eventually they would wonder why the tall lanky one at the back was there when she couldn't sing or dance. It wasn't for lack of trying. Every Saturday I went to dance class in the city. Street dance, tap, jazz AND funk, if you must know. Our teacher Daire was a ride and as I have never particularly enjoyed dancing, I mainly went along to stare at him. I also went to singing lessons, but at all these classes there were people who were so much better than me, which made me feel even shitter than I actually was. Clearly, some level of confidence was at play though, for me to keep bringing myself to auditions. I'd turn up and sing Alicia Keys – God forbid I'd start with something easy. I'm surprised I didn't waltz in with Mariah Carey ready to go.

It was a fun time in my life and I did feel like I was attempting something of a career, especially after I got spotted in fifth year and asked to be in a L'Oréal hair show. BIG MISTAKE. If you ever find yourself being asked to be in a hair show, run. My God, two years it took to get some kind of normal hairstyle back. They cut it into a V at the back and thinned it out, even though it was already violently thin. They then dyed it red and blonde and oh! the pièce de résistance, a massive fringe that started from behind my ears. Imagine trying to grow that yoke out? My big modelling debut ended up being me walking around looking like Worzel Gummidge or a member of The Cure.

At the time though, it didn't matter; I was young enough to think I was deadly, and even if they did take the head off me, that could not distract from the fact that I had the right to call myself a model because I was on a runway. When my hair finally did start to grow back I chucked a load of clip-in extensions into my head, which meant I ended up looking like MacGyver for most of fifth year and sixth year, which was unfortunate because I was so rotten in first year and felt like I had really turned a corner looks-wise. But it was back to square one for Big Mouth.

Come to think of it, it was around this time I met my first proper boyfriend. I had first spotted him in a pub in Howth, The Bloody Stream, which is under the Dart station; this was back when my fake passport opened up doors I never imagined, The Bloody Stream being one of them. (I knew a guy who made fake passports. He belonged on the dark web and not in his mother's basement.) There were a few weekends of staring involved, and then myself and my pal were invited to some of his and his friend's parties, which we were more than willing to go to. At twenty-five he was a lot older than I was and it took an awful lot of me pursuing him, but I kinda got my hands on him for a while. I didn't fall in love with him but I was mad about him and the fact that he was older than me made him even more appealing. When we met he had just broken up with his long-term girlfriend and eventually he dumped me and got back with her. Not to show off, but I've only been dumped once in my life and it was by him. I've been ghosted and there was the silly teenage stuff but being properly dumped was a new experience. But who can blame him? That haircut and the audition for the fast-food ad I went to probably spelled the end for us.

At the audition I had to kiss someone, but being new to the game I assumed they meant full-on kiss, so I went in and practically ate the male lead's head off. Didn't even get the role – apparently they wanted more of a peck on the cheek than the pornographic scenes I was delivering. On with my quest I continued all the same, not one to give up easily. I added a lot of acting courses to my dance and singing lessons and mastered the art of being an orange. Why do they always want you to be an orange? Come to think of it, my parents must have really wanted me out of the house a fair bit because they always paid for my courses. One summer I even got to go to London on a Shakespeare-based acting course with RADA and Anthony Hopkins attended RADA, I will have you know. Did I mention I went to RADA? I had no idea this would be all sword fighting (the word 'Shakespeare' gave nothing away to me), so it was an unusual way to spend a summer. Thankfully, I had discovered poppers at that stage and they made the whole adventure quite a bit more interesting.

As I was getting into my later teenage years the rules at home in Howth were getting harder to follow. I still wasn't allowed out to see my friends during the week and absolutely no drinking of alcohol was allowed. Get a grip, Sandra. After the local nightclub I had to be home by 1 a.m. and if I was even a minute late the front door was locked and then I was in serious trouble. That wasn't for me. The nightclub in question was the one I mentioned earlier, K2, and it was up the summit in Howth. It was for eighteen-year-olds only, unless you knew someone who made fake IDs, which of course I did and had many. (You needed a few because sometimes they got taken away by the bouncer.)

Everyone else's parents seemed much less strict than mine. One summer I went on holiday with a friend and her parents were total sounders, letting us get hammered and stay out until 6 a.m. I knew this wasn't going to be repeated by my parents when she came away with us, but I thought we would still have fun. We did not. She eventually got her aunt to pick her up and take her to her house in Spain. The strict parents strike again. On skiing holidays there was the strict condition that we hit the slopes as soon as the lifts opened at 8 a.m. Crawling out of bed, definitely still drunk, was not fun. I remember being in the queue at the ski lift eating the snow off my snowboard because the hangover thirst was so intense. One morning Neil caught us all snoozing and World War Three erupted, much the same as when we ordered more chips at dinner and never ate them. The man does NOT like waste.

One year I snuck down to Oxygen, which was our big summer festival at the time (although it never felt very summery because it would lash rain all weekend long). I wasn't allowed to go, which was fair enough considering I was sixteen, but I went anyway and got away with it. All of my pals were allowed to go, but my parents knew I would abuse the freedom and I certainly did that. When I got there, I bumped into Amber, who looked like she had drunk all of the alcohol at the festival, a common theme among us at festivals and a little tradition we like to carry on. Medical tent, see you soon my friend!

For a whole summer my best pal Ashley and I went through a phase of drinking as often as we could, even though we hadn't a penny to our names. (Some nights we would find ourselves in an early house – pubs that opened at 5 a.m. for fishermen who had come in off sea – two broke sea creatures hanging around to see who might offer to buy them a drink.) On the off chance we had money it would be fistfuls of coins that we would pool together and buy anything we could, usually a bottle of wine that tasted like vinegar. One night we brought the wine back to Ashley's dad's house to drink. Derek (her dad) was in at the time and Ashley had promised that there was no way he would have a glass of wine if we offered it, but we should be polite and at least offer. We begrudgingly offered Derek some wine and to our shock and horror he accepted – he got the smallest glass of wine he would ever be so unlucky to receive. I couldn't forgive Ashley until we had gotten suitably drunk after finishing the rest of the bottle.

Before my twenty-five-year-old boyfriend and I broke up, Ashley and I were in her bedroom (probably hiding from her dad in case he asked for some of our precious wine), discussing his friend who I was also interested in. This lad was even older, so even more appealing. During our chat I called my boyfriend but he didn't answer. What I didn't realise was that it had gone to voicemail so he heard an entire pros and cons conversation involving him and his pal – in my defence he was losing interest in me, which made me determined to lose interest in him rather than lose face! I doubt he gave a shit though, because the list was pathetic. 'Okay, so he works a lot so can't give me as many lifts as his friend can.' 'He's a bit small and his friend is better looking.' (That one might have hurt.) I can still picture myself and Ashley sitting in her room, Asho furiously agreeing with what I was saying, as all good friends do …

Still, that was a tough one to live down because I really don't ever like making anyone feel bad about themselves and it was a moment of bitchiness that should never have been heard. (Whenever I see a fifty-year-old Leonardo DiCaprio going out with a girl in their twenties, I always think the same thing: you simply don't have the same maturity levels of someone a lot older, nor are you overly interested in what they are talking about.) Looking back I can see why he dumped me; it must have become boring. I started to act my age and he thought, I'm out!

Not long after the break-up my mom was driving me home from school and we ended up stuck in traffic behind him and his new/old girlfriend. I was very upset having to watch them kiss each other in the car in front while pretending to my mom that I was fine, although she wouldn't have given a shite anyway. My mother had very little time for my heartbreak and still doesn't. Years later at her fiftieth birthday party I was having myself a massive pity party because I had just broken up with my long-term boyfriend. She wasn't having anyone stealing her thunder and screeched at me to cop on. I cried and cried and still got zero sympathy, so I gave up and started milling into the free booze with Amber.

In our house it was Frederick who got away with EVERYTHING. He threw wild parties – pool parties with about twenty friends – and never got caught. I would arrive home from being out with my friends and he would shout at me and make me go to my room if I so much as glanced at his friends. (There was only one of them I wanted to kiss and I did in the end but I had to wait until I moved to London out of reach of Rico because that was exactly what he was trying to avoid me doing.) One morning I went in to wake him and almost died when I saw his face. The night before he had gotten hammered and decided the best way to get home was to cycle – DERANGED. He had taken a lump out of the skin between his lip and his nose and he still has a scar there today.

Eventually Frederick went too far when he wedged my mom's car on the cliffs in Howth. He was allowed to drive Mom and Neil's cars because at one point (hard to believe now), he was their favourite child – I really have no idea how he snuck into that role! Rico and his pal Sean thought it would be fun to see if my mom's sports car could drive up the cliffs. It couldn't and the fire brigade was called swiftly by my mother who went SPARE. Rico. What a dope.

Even after he nearly totalled Mom's car, they still bought him his own one. Both Amber and Frederick were given cars but as usual I had done something to piss Neil and Sandra off, so I wasn't on the car list. They said my dad could get me one, but I couldn't park it near the house (they didn't like my dad) so it was basically impossible for me. It was easier to scab lifts – cheaper too. A couple of Rico's friends were my drivers/pals and would give me lifts everywhere, which was very handy considering I didn't have a car. It was a great exchange: I would provide fantastic company and they would give me a lift. One of Frederick's friends got me into rap music, which is still to this day my favourite music to listen to. Eventually my dad did buy me my first car. It was my dream car, a Peugeot 206 in mint green, and I was thrilled. The downside was that because my dad was a used car salesman at any point the car could be sold … and it was. He then got me a burnt orange Skoda Fabia in its place and instead of being grateful I was horrified. I wrote it off not long after, not on purpose, but he wasn't so quick to change my car after that incident.

My parents' divorce was something I had learned to use to my advantage from a very young age and I used it a lot to find a way around my mom's rules. It was very simple: I went to my dad's house. Freddie was GREAT craic and I could get him to allow me to do most things by saying Mom let me do them; they didn't speak so it wasn't like he could fact-check me. I can't say he was great at organising dinner for when I got home from school, but I loved a Chinese takeaway so it worked well.

These were the finer parts of divorce, which I thoroughly enjoyed; on the one hand we had a magnificent house in Howth with Mom and Neil and everything we could want, but they were very strict. My dad's house wasn't as picture perfect as my mom's, but I loved it because I was allowed my freedom there, which is what you really want as a teenager. I guess I model my own parenting style off both of my upbringings, trying to give my kids the best of both worlds; a little bit of freedom mixed with some routine.

When I was seventeen, Sandra and Neil kicked me out, which was totally deserved, so I went to live full-time with my dad. Mom had reached the end of her wick and had it up to there with me. My relationship with my mom was pretty strained by this time; I never really considered her a friend growing up and could never imagine that ever changing. We didn't spend much time together outside of the house, had very separate lives and a lot of ups and downs on account of me being an asshole to be around. It was hard for us to connect because I was difficult and there was a fair bit of drama with me seeing my dad. That upset her and she didn't know how to be anything but bothered by me.

Freddie was great but wasn't used to having a teenager living with him so his routine stayed mostly the same. He would drop me to school and I would rarely see him until late that night as he would be in the pub until around nine. Because I could forge my dad's signature, I would take a day off school when I felt it was needed. Whenever Naomi was onto me, I'd ring my dad and tell him I would be expelled if he didn't say he wrote the note. Poor Naomi, she once followed me out of the school gates asking me not to go home early, but I insisted I had a note and very good reason to be leaving (an arranged meet-up with the boys from the school down the road).

A friend of mine who lived up the road from my dad's house would come over after school and we would get hammered in the front room, drink all of my dad's booze and smoke his Benson & Hedges cigarettes. When my dad arrived home, we'd push the couch against the door and I would shout that my pal was naked so he couldn't come in. Never once did he ask why my pal was naked; he just left us to it. (She wasn't naked by the way, we just had a lot more booze to get through.) I went turbo on his booze trolley because I knew the chances of him noticing were slim; in fact my Dad never noticed that he was drinking a lot of water and coke at home.

At night we used to climb out of my window and sneak off to a nightclub up the road: Tamangos where the gang goes (great tagline, great nightclub). It was such bad behaviour but we had the time of our lives. We had no money so would scab drinks off people and there were probably some drink robberies going on in the club too: if you put your drink down and took your eyes off it, there was a strong possibility that I or my friend would have nicked it.

Dad used to leave his front door open – he thought nobody would burgle the house because they would assume someone was home. It doesn't work like that and he was robbed quite a few times. He always left piles of cash around and I should know this because some of that cash would fall into the wrong hands (mine, basically). On two occasions men using syringes came to rob his house. Those idiots didn't realise I'd already taken all the cash. (Well, not all of it; unfortunately, I had left loads for the professional robbers.) Another time I rang him and pretended the house had been robbed, only for him to rush home to find me and my pal rolling around laughing on his front lawn. Well worth getting in trouble for to see the look on his face. I loved nothing more than pranking my dad and he always saw the funny side. Eventually.

As far as I could tell, my dad never slept. If I crept into his house late at night, he would always shout my name as I was coming up the stairs. I would peer into his room and see a lit cigarette (he never smoked with the light on, just aimed the ash at where the ashtray was). I think his leg gave him a lot of pain and kept him awake. My dad was sick and in and out of hospital most of my life. He did cause most of his problems through smoking and drinking, but in the same breath he couldn't help it so it wasn't his fault. The man used to put butter on his chips and have four takeaways a week – gout became an almost permanent fixture of his body. Who gets gout? People who put butter on their chips, that's who. (Although I'm not a medical professional so don't quote me on that.) When I was eight he had two heart attacks in two days, one of which happened in one of his favourite pubs, the Stoop Your Head in Skerries. He insisted on staying there until my cousin Jeff dragged him out of the place and drove him to hospital. When I went in to see him I had my Game Boy with me; I looked up at him as I walked into the room and got such a fright that I wouldn't look at him again. He was hooked up to the most insane amount of wires and breathing stuff. Thank God for Mario Kart because it was easy enough to ignore him with that in my hands.

As we got older my siblings and I became more involved in his health struggles and at times it did feel annoying to us, which is a terrible thing to say, but it's also true and to a point fair. To amuse ourselves we would make a lot of late-night phone calls to his hospital bed. I'm ashamed to say these were not check-ins but very drunk 3 a.m. phone calls, thinking we were being hilarious disturbing him from his sleep. But I don't think he minded, he honestly loved chatting to us. Sure, what else would you be doing in Beaumont Hospital? I certainly kept him company and there was never, ever a missed call; he always answered no matter what, because on some level he must have found it entertaining. We loved him giving out to us because he was never serious. I reckon I could have done absolutely anything and he wouldn't have batted an eyelid. Hospital is also a very boring place, particularly when you are there for so long – sometimes he'd be there for three months at a time. What's a late-night phone call in the grand scheme of things?

Chapter Six

Hello Wall

If you're not Irish you may not get the significance of a sixth-year holiday, but it's a rite of passage for many of us when we finish the Leaving Certificate exams in our sixth and final year of school. For the most part I had loved school, but by eighteen it was definitely time to move onto the next stage of my life (I wanted to study Architecture at Trinity College Dublin). The idea of the sixth-year holiday is to celebrate the end of school by going away to a holiday complex (because that's all you can afford) somewhere hot with all your friends, a pack of teenage Shirley Valentines, to spend all your money on cheap booze. Sounds like a lot of fun even now, and it was.

My boyfriend at the time didn't come with me and although it wasn't very serious, we were, in fairness, meant to be exclusive. Until I spotted a ride in Greece and, after having a private discussion with myself, decided that for that night my relationship at home was not exclusive. The next day I woke up full of fear and regret, keeping in mind I had only kissed this fella, I was still in my frigid era (there has yet to be another era but I hold out hope). My friends made it worse and insisted I call my boyfriend to tell him the bad news. He didn't dump me but soon realised I wasn't that into him if I was up to this kind of messing on holidays. Readers, don't always do what your pals tell you to, they are not always right. I would have been perfectly comfortable not telling him and I think he would have preferred not to know. That's the thing about cheating, I'm not sure it's always a good idea to tell the person because if you deeply regret what you've done, will never do it again and know that your significant other will never find out, is there any reason to hurt them? In some circumstances, though, I do think people tell their significant other to ease their guilt and their pain and I am certain I would be one of those people. In many a dream I have run screaming and crying to tell Spen what I've been up to. Cheating dreams are the worst; whether it's me cheating on someone or me being cheated on, I always wake up with a lot of panic from both scenarios and can never decide which one is worse.

Back from Greece it was time to collect our exam results and see what college courses we'd been accepted to. In school I thought I was a real clever clogs, but the problem with thinking you're really clever and immune to any need to study is that you are very likely to fuck things up, which I did. The maximum number of points you can get in the Irish Leaving Certificate is 625 and I needed a cool 486 to study Architecture at Trinity College. The madness of me thinking I would get 486 points! You have to admire the confidence though. Instead I got 300 points and none of the courses I applied to. What a gobshite! Ah well, school was officially over and I had a party to get ready for.

After you finish school in Ireland the most important part of your social calendar for the year is your Debs (like a prom in the UK and US). The Debs is an end of summer ball that is organised by the year heads and students and is a very important thing to happen to your eighteen-year-old self. I could not wait! My dress – the most important thing to ever exist – took me a long time to procure and my mom actually spent a bit of money on it, which was very unusual for her. (She certainly wouldn't repeat that now. My brother just turned thirty and assumed he would get a decent present, not knowing Sandra had already been to Zara to buy him a 30-euro jumper – 30 quid for 30 years is her motto, unless of course she is buying something for herself!) Anyway, I found my dream dress in Spain and MY GOD did that dress do the rounds among my friends. I wouldn't have been surprised if it had just melted away by the end, such was the extent of the amount of people borrowing it. The shop in Spain was very cool and chic and not somewhere I would have normally found myself so I spent hours in there trying on dresses, even though I knew which one I was going to get from the moment I walked in. On dress try number seven hundred and sixty-eight I looked down and noticed something really weird stuck in the very tight dress I was wearing. After much investigation we figured out a cockroach had lodged itself in the dress that was now on my body – I have never whipped my clothes off faster. My mother found this hilarious; I was terrified but still wanted the dress – preferably without the cockroach and with a heavy discount. Ugh, thinking back cock-roaches lay eggs so it's possible I took an entire cockroach family to my Debs!

Next up I had to book in my hair and make-up. The only option for me was the MAC counter because at the time they applied more make-up than every other make-up brand combined and that's the look I was going for. To top it off my quiff was huge and my shoes made me look like a giraffe. Perfect.

The usual thing to do was to invite your boyfriend to the Debs and I did have a boyfriend at the time, but he wasn't as much craic as my good friend Reds (Conor – he has red hair so has always been called that). To me the obvious thing to do was to invite Reds, so I did. Sandra found out and thought I was being a mean little bitch (in hindsight, I was) and made me uninvite Reds and invite my boyfriend instead. We started the night with drinks in my friend Clodagh's house – her parents were the sound ones so we knew we would get away with plenty of drinks. After what seemed like hours of taking photos of each other, the girls and our dates headed off into the night in our big white limo, absolutely thrilled with ourselves. (It was essential to go in a big white limo to a night I can only describe as a very budget wedding.) The hotel was extremely basic – the function room was just a very badly decorated room – but it was perfect. We all sat down to a three-course meal of soggy potatoes and grey meat but I ate very little and instead focused my energies on spending all the money my parents had given me on vodka. There was dancing for sure, but as always I avoided it like the plague, even when my date asked me to dance. I was at the stage where I thought dancing with someone was the most embarrassing thing I had ever heard of. Oh what a night! So many fallen sixth-years puking in the toilets – a great night had by all! Miraculously, despite all the vodka, I made it out alive and off we went into the night for more revelry, although I have no clue where. All I know is I got home at 4 a.m. and stuffed my face with a beige platter of waffles and chicken nuggets.

After I got over the disappointment of only getting 300 points, I had a quick chat with my pals and it was decided that if I couldn't study Architecture at Trinity then I would do a PLC (Post Leaving Certificate) course in Dublin in Real Estate. It didn't matter that I had less than zero interest in selling property; it was going to serve the purpose of getting me into Architecture, which is what I was sure I wanted to do. This plan was going perfectly until Neil found out. He very kindly – but with an undertone of 'you've got two options' – told me that he had gotten me on a course in Aberdeen at Robert Gordon University. The course was construction design and management and there was a flight leaving Monday morning. If I went Neil said he would cover my costs. The alternative was that I move out, get a job and pay my own way fully.

Neil was always insistent that we got degree; it was as if he believed we would die if we didn't get one. He used to be a teacher so I guess education was of the utmost importance to him but I think you can do most things without a degree. Now, I probably wouldn't trust a doctor who didn't have one, but besides that you're golden. I took Neil's money and ran straight to Aberdeen. Well, I didn't run, I hopped on a Ryanair flight with all my crap, knowing I would have to make this journey countless times. I was very upset on that flight, but I knew I only had myself to blame.

Aberdeen is called the granite city because all the buildings are made of granite. Even though I'd grown up around Scottish people I hadn't a clue what a lot of people I met were saying and I did have the odd cry on the phone to my mom … Cen fit like men fits the storr-rrrrryyyyyyyy. Sorry Fraser, are you asking for another drink because I haven't any idea what you're trying to say to me? (This was a phrase I heard all the time, apparently it means 'How's it going?') It was also cold, very cold, and this cold combined with the permanent grey skies and buildings meant you could find yourself longing for a Caribbean island. But it's also a beautiful place with the most amazing countryside and great people.

Looking back it's mad that I went to uni in Aberdeen because I was such a home bird at the time. Although, full transparency, Amber and Frederick were also studying there. They had a flat together and I could have lived with them but chose to live with my pals instead so I can't have been that homesick! Frederick was studying Architecture and Amber had just begun her path of the eternal student – altogether she spent seven years at uni over there. Whenever the idea of leaving and getting a job came up, she suddenly found yet another course she would love.

When I first arrived I moved into uni halls, but my Aunty Lexi came to settle me in and thank God she did because she rang her brother Neil and told him I couldn't stay in that dump. It was the same place that Amber and

Frederick had stayed in their first years, but Lexi told Neil it was too rotten for me. Instead I moved to nicer student accommodation with my own bathroom and shower. I got on really well with one of the girls I was staying with and we made a few other friends from the flat across the way.

I used to smoke back then, thinking I was cool, and would sit down to a huge bowl of Corn Pops and a cigarette for breakfast at the same time. Disgusting. I will never forget when my roommate's parents came to visit and we had the pizza situation. She had her family over for pizza and a catch-up, mum, dad, sister – all sound, lovely people. When I came home, after they had eaten, to my horror I saw my bathroom scissors sitting on the kitchen counter. (There are bathroom scissors and there are kitchen scissors and the two should NEVER be mixed up.) I felt sick. My nail and trimming scissors for any and all body hair had walked themselves into the kitchen where they had no business being. It turns out some families cut pizzas with scissors and my pube scissors were the ones of choice that day. I wish I could say I didn't have the heart to tell her but it was just too funny and I couldn't help myself. Her parents never found out, which was the main thing, and my scissors never left the bathroom again!

My allowance was £100 a week and as I only ever ate pasta pesto, I was able to stretch it quite far. (Pasta pesto is still one of my favourite meals.) I went wild in Aberdeen:

it's a huge student city and I loved partying. A vodka mix was only £1 in our local uni bar and there was always someone to go out with, so it suited me down to the ground. My class was mostly boys, which was fine, but I didn't get on particularly well with any of them except Steve, who became my best pal. Steve was a mature student and was great craic. He used to call me his shadow because I just followed him around everywhere like a little puppy. One great thing about Aberdeen was that all the big DJs would come and play – Felix da Housecat, Dave Clarke, Green Velvet – so I was in my element. My pals would come over from Ireland sometimes and we would truly lose our minds. One night I was at the front of the crowd at Felix, practically touching the man, and he gave me his sweat towel as a gift. I shudder at the thought now, but back then I thought I was deadly and took it home with me. That stinky towel stayed with me until the end of that year, although I forgot all about it until I found it rotting at the bottom of my wardrobe on move-out day.

At the time Amber was doing the first of her many degrees and only had two hours of uni a week. My course was 9–5 each day so I felt very hard done by. We decided we needed jobs and got one together in the local Wetherspoons; they paid us nothing and we worked our asses off. All the broke students went to Wetherspoons so working there was kind of like being out for the night.

Amber quit soon enough; she was smart and decided she'd rather get by on our allowance but because I really love clothes, I wanted the extra money to buy some so I found a job in a restaurant. It was a high-end restaurant – not London high-end but pricey enough – and I've never had worse tips in my life. A family of four used to come in and spend a tonne of money on their food but leave a 20p tip or whatever they had in their pocket, never over a quid. I learned a valuable lesson then: always tip and tip well if you can. Leaving someone 20p is insulting when you've been waited on hand and foot.

Dating was fun in Aberdeen but I didn't take it too seriously because I couldn't wait to get back to Dublin. At that time all I wanted was to be at home in Ireland with my friends, but looking back Aberdeen was actually a brilliant and fun place to be at uni, something I never thought I would say! In Aberdeen I had a couple of boyfriends but this was during my indie phase and good God, were they in bits. They didn't have much personality either but my pals thought they were cool because they were in bands, so I did too. I also went out with a chef – he wasn't much of a looker but on the plus side he had a good personality and I worked with him so logistically it was handy. In general my taste doesn't usually equate to 'ride', but I must take into account that my husband is a ride. (God, I hope he doesn't read that, I'm trying to tone down his self-love!)

One fella I went out with was absolutely mad about himself. He was the first guy I'd ever been with that was ripped, but he plucked his eyebrows to within an inch of their lives so they were like two little lines above his eyes. I'd never have gotten away with dating him in Ireland, but I wasn't in Ireland, I was in Scotland, and sure nobody would know, so I said, 'Fuck it.' Because I only ever saw him when I was very drunk, I didn't notice the manicured brows too often, but looking back they were a huge red flag.

The situation came to what I thought was a natural end, but he wasn't too pleased about it, which I thought was strange because we only ever saw each other on nights out. Now and then he would call over to my house after we broke up; once he left me a massive jar of orange Smarties. This was back in the day when you couldn't buy packs of orange Smarties (the best one), so he had gone to the trouble of picking out the orange ones for me. Romance isn't dead! It was very sweet; he knocked on our door and then ran away but he had left a note professing how much he liked me. It was great entertainment for us that afternoon, but I still didn't want to get back with him so that was the end of that, and yes, of course, I did eat all the Smarties.

One fella I dated was a trainee doctor from Derry, who I worked with in Wetherspoons, the place where all good romances start. He didn't show too much interest in me to begin with so I liked him even more; plus he would be able to write me prescriptions when he passed his exams so I was looking out for my future self. He was a really nice guy, actually; I wonder what he's up to now? I often think about people I used to know and wonder if they're dead or not – a strange way to think, I know, but it's where my mind travels to. The night before I went home for Christmas, he was working a shift and we planned to meet up when he'd finished. Unfortunately, that night I drank too much wine and I fell asleep, missing all his calls. It fizzled out after that and I blamed the wine, which I've rarely touched since. I do miss a Derry accent though.

Wow. Before writing this book I would have said I went out with very few people – I must have blocked a lot of them out! I never wanted to be a 'relationship' girl, but that's just the way it's turned out and relationships have taken many years of my life. I do often wonder why it's been this way. Very possibly I should have gotten out and about more, if you get my drift (my mother will read this), but it just never happened that way. I would kiss anyone you put in front of me (well, almost anyone), but anything more intimate requires a really good connection and for me it takes time to build that.

Chapter Seven

I'm a Builder

During the summer holidays between first and second year of college in Aberdeen I did my J-1 summer with Johanna, a good friend from secondary school. (A J-1 is a visa that lets you work in the US for a few months in the summer.) Johanna and I were great drinking buddies at school. We once sat in her driveway for an hour talking absolute shite after stumbling home from the pub until her sister screamed at us because she was sitting some very important exams the next day. Our party of two moved indoors and we had to sesh in the dark very quietly so her sister couldn't hear us.

We went to Chicago first. We had no jobs lined up, but friends of ours from Howth had rented a squat-like house and gave us a room there. We could have worked in a hotel but for some reason they all required a drug test, which we weren't willing to do. We didn't smoke weed (I never really got the vibe of that) but the boys we lived with always did and we were paranoid about second-hand inhalation, thinking that if we tested positive, we would be deported and thrown into jail somewhere awful.

Eventually we got a job handing out fliers. The first morning we were handing out fliers at 7 a.m. when the owner of the company just happened to walk by. We decided that was enough to convince him we were very diligent so we went back to the squat, stored the fliers away and went back to bed, never to take to the streets again. Later he came to one of our parties and we were petrified he would find the fliers but he never did. I still feel guilty about that to this day.

We were loose animals that summer and so broke that we would take ourselves to the supermarket and just walk around eating the food: yoghurts, packets of ham and crackers; this way it didn't feel like stealing. One of us did manage to swipe a 3-litre bottle of vodka and I think even the store owner would have been impressed with that. From Chicago we headed off to San Francisco where my dad's friend Swiggy had gotten me a job as a hostess in the Nob Hill Café. I loved it there and after I got over the initial hilarity of the name I got to work. It was a very cool place to be – there was always a queue to get in. I was a hostess and had never earned money quite like it. (Abercrombie & Fitch didn't know what hit it; by the time I was heading home my suitcase was bulging with clothes.)

Regulars at the café were twins and retired TV actresses Marian and Vivienne. They were famous in San Fran and people would come in and ask for pictures with them. They must have been in their eighties at the time I worked there but they were always dressed to the nines. My favourite of their looks was matching leopard-print coats with identical cowboy hats. Each time they came in they would sit in the same seat, eat the same food and they always dressed the same. Always. Everything was identical about them; apparently in their house they had two single beds in one room with matching duvets. They were two divas who wanted things the way they wanted them and fair enough; looking that fabulous, who was I to question them?

We lived with the owner of the café. Carol, who was in her seventies, was so cool and had a cat called Sambuca. Every night she would fall asleep with the TV on full volume and would wake intermittently, calling out for her beloved Sambuca. Her kids were not in line for sainthood either, so I dare say she enjoyed our company and it didn't take long for her to shout at us if we pissed her off. She let me, Johanna, Amber and Lynn stay in her house all summer, free of charge. An angel. Luckily, her hearing wasn't great. Sometimes her son would take us out to these wild parties and we would take full advantage.

He and his friends once made the mistake of inviting us to their friend's fortieth party in a winery in Sacramento. We all got so drunk, but in our defence, they gave us mimosas at 9 a.m., so what did they expect? We all got kicked out. Strangely enough they still thought we were fun and continued to invite us out with them even after that, the mad bastards.

Our first night ever in a karaoke bar was in San Francisco and our song of choice was 'Cocaine' by Eric Clapton – we thought we were absolutely gas. Oh, the fun we had on that trip. Looking back I can't believe how lucky I was to be able to live over there at that age, experiencing a completely different kind of life and so much more freedom than I'd ever had at home. Strangely enough, considering I'd felt a lot like a caged bull growing up, always raring to get out of the pen and cause mayhem wherever I went, I was more well-behaved than I expected. Not that I was first in line for being good or anything, but it really could have been a lot worse. Amber and I even managed to do some touristy things while in San Fran; we visited the seals at the harbour and did a night excursion to Alcatraz, which I loved – mainly because I never, ever want to be in jail – but still, I'm nosy and loved having a snoop around.

One weekend Carol took us to a place called the Russian River and on the way there we stopped at a BBQ place, which I will never forget; to this day it's my dream meal. We didn't do much at the river except swim and (of course) drink. She had a house there that was about to fall down and I'm surprised it didn't; it was a full knock-and-rebuild job. On our first night we were woken up by two bats – I personally don't mind a bat but I'd rather one didn't end up in my hair. Amber very bravely guided them out of there, but let's just say we weren't exactly in a mad rush to go back to the Russian River again after that.

One of my favourite things to do in San Fran was to wander around the city; I felt very grown-up and had cash to burn with my hostessing job. My desire to save money hadn't kicked in back then and if I ever ran out of it you could be sure Freddie was getting a call and it was off to the Western Union to collect it. (I'm pretty sure I called him even when I hadn't run out of money too.) We soon made friends with some Irish lads, because naturally that's what you do when you move anywhere outside of Ireland: you look for Irish people. They were renting out rooms in a frat house in Berkeley and threw these insane parties. Most weekends we would get the train (the BART) to Berkeley, then wake up the next day with violent hangovers, but the parties were amazing – exactly what you would imagine from a frat house, hundreds of people in this insane student pit. The place was filthy and even back then I knew better than to touch any of their glasses – plastic cups only please (back in those days we didn't know plastic was killing our planet).

Before one of these parties Amber had just returned to San Fran from Thailand and was making her way over to us from the airport with some Thai whiskey, which we'd heard could send the most sane person insane – we couldn't wait. Off we went for another weekend in the frat house, a very tired and jet-lagged Amber in tow with the whiskey. Things were going well but poor Ambi very quickly turned into a fallen soldier. I remember we locked her in a room to sleep it off. LOCKED HER IN A ROOM! Locked. A. Drunk. Person. In. A. Room. How on earth any of us survived our teenage years I will never know.

We gave nicknames to some of the boys. One of them we called Wanky because one of the girls had said he was always asking for one but without much luck (it was actually Winky Wanky because his member was not of the large variety). I took a shine to one of the lads and actually ended up meeting him in Dublin. When I invited him to Howth for a party, he came to our apartment and naturally what happens in Howth is that you get invited to another party, but he didn't want to go to that party so off I went without him. Upon my return I found that he had left in a rage and because I hadn't stayed and gone to bed with him (something I had never had any intention of doing), he'd squirted ketchup in my shoes and my toaster, what a sap. Anyway, pre the ketchup revenge those boys had been sound.

When I came back to Dublin after that trip, I met someone I fell in love with and was with for over six years. It was my first long-term relationship, but it was very on and off the whole way through. We met when I was working at an event holding trays of drinks – my wrists were in bits because nobody seemed to be drinking that evening. When I spotted my soon-to-be boyfriend, I couldn't take my eyes off him; I didn't give a shite about the drinks or the job after that. Instead I spent the entire evening staring at him until he eventually came over and started talking to me; it could have gone either way because I did look like a total weirdo staring at him. It genuinely felt like love at first sight and I had never really had that before. He asked for my number and it was lucky he did because I got sent home shortly after, mainly because I wasn't doing the job I was being paid to do.

At that time I really hadn't done much dating; I'd had boyfriends but it was all very teenager-y, usually meeting up in a pub or club with friends for a few drinks. So when he rang and asked me out I kept making up excuses; I was really nervous and didn't want to go – but also *really* wanted to go. Eventually after three tries I met up with him and he told me that was going to have been his last attempt because I kept saying no. Soon after that I bumped into him everywhere, including at Daft Punk in Marley Park, still the best gig of my life. After the concert we went back to his house for a party and that was that, we were a couple.

When I start a new relationship I always have a lot of fun – I guess alcohol makes me less shy. He was a graffiti artist and would occasionally take me 'tagging' with him. I turned into quite the vandal, although I was better at holding the cans of paint than the painting. When the summer ended I had to go back to Aberdeen for my second and final year of college, but I flew home to see him every chance I got and he even made the trip over to see me. Long distance is very hard work for any relationship and we would end up having the most pointless fights.

As I was coming up to the end of my course I could taste the freedom. The final stage of it was to find a work placement and I found one in London. THE DREAM! My boyfriend was not impressed but I'm still quite proud that I went to London and didn't stay at home for a boy, albeit a boy I was crazy about. The chance to live in London was too much of a pull for me. Of course, I never considered that living in London on the suggestion of a salary from a placement would be difficult, but luckily it was Neil to the rescue again and he offered to pay for my accommodation. I had hated him for sending me to Aberdeen, but to be fair everything led onto the next thing.

There were over two thousand applicants for the placement working as a site engineer in FF&E (fixtures, fittings and electrical) for a large construction company. When I walked into the interview the first thing they asked me was why I wanted a job in FF&E. I did not have a clue about FF&E (I only knew I wanted to go raving in London very badly), but for the purpose of the interview I somehow managed to describe why I loved FF&E so much, despite not having any idea what it was. 'So, Vogue, why the interest in FF&E?' they asked me. 'Well, you see, ever since I was young I always had a fascination with it, it just stuck out to me. Then I began my degree and it further cemented [little building pun] the fact that my true goal was to work on FF&E. It's not for everyone but let me tell you it's definitely for me and if you hire me I won't let you down!'

In the bag! I couldn't believe it (although I was less excited after I googled FF&E). Do I feel slightly guilty about the other poor applicants who actually *did* want that job and not just to live and rave in London? Yes, I do now, but I was so thrilled to be moving to London that I didn't dwell on it at the time.

Nobody had told me how vast London is and when my pal offered me a place to live in Stockwell I took it. It was only after I moved in that I discovered that I'd be commuting an hour and a half to and from work every single day. Well, not every day because, obviously, partying was important so I missed more Mondays than I should have. (I also missed the day after St Patrick's day, which was a difficult one to cover up!) My first job on my first day was to get measurements for where the toilets and sinks should go. My boss looked perplexed at the figures I returned with and immediately knew he had made a mistake … the new FF&E lover couldn't even measure up. Uh oh!

It got better from there on, but they still had to bribe me to go on site by letting me choose my own steel-capped boots. I was thrilled at the thought of picking out a chic, steel-capped boot until I opened the building supplies magazine – all rotten, very sturdy shoes you might imagine a person of the cloth wearing. For the most part I much preferred the indoor work but, strangely enough, when May came around and the sun was shining, I found being out on site so much more suitable. I'd say the older gentlemen working there must have been only too thrilled to see me every day in my hand-picked steel-capped shoes, looking the part but not quite acting it. But I was a quick learner and was kept very busy. As a site engineer I had many roles, including inducting all new employees and giving them a safety briefing. I really tried to be assertive so people would take me seriously and I have to say, for a very big company, they let me do a lot of important contractual work. But as I was the only woman the lads' humour did get a bit boring after a while. One day I spent a couple of hours in a digger because one of them thought it was gas to lock me in – and it would have been gas too, had it not been me.

After work was another story. London was so much fun and I was living with two Irish girls who, like me, really enjoyed a party. When we left that apartment our landlord kept our deposit, the little snake. He had checked our Facebook pages and found pictures of us dancing on our stage (his built-in cupboards). The fantastic stage performances we put on were worth the money though, and living there really helped me come out of my shell.

When my six-month placement ended I wasn't offered a job, which came as no great surprise. As much as I had enjoyed London, I still really wanted to go home to Ireland. The price for that was another degree to keep my parents off my back – in quantity surveying. It's a bit like being an accountant for concrete and was unbelievably boring. All my life I've recoiled at the mere mention of numbers so it really wasn't my calling, but I stuck it out because it meant I could go back to Dublin, do my pretend modelling at the same time and be with my boyfriend, who I had been missing a lot by this point. So all good!

Chapter Eight

State of Yer One

An agent once told me that if I wanted to succeed as a model I had to stop eating burgers, but I was happy with my little modelling spot in Ireland that still allowed me to indulge. Anyway, it's Chinese food that has always been my downfall – it's a good job spice bags* weren't around when I was younger. I always use the term 'modelling' loosely because a lot of the time I was standing on the busiest shopping street in Dublin holding a Magnum ice cream in a bikini or promoting something else with very few clothes on. Even though my modelling career wasn't very glamorous there were always a lot of 'who does she think she is' vibes that went with it – people assumed I thought I was deadly, which is a big no-no in

* The spice bag is probably Ireland's favourite takeaway dish, consisting of crispy fried chicken, peppers, chilli and chips, all seasoned in a bag.

Ireland: 'The state of her, she's no model!' Dead right, I certainly was not, but in fairness to the haters I did have notions! I once went into Storm modelling agency thinking they would represent me. It was polite no and off I trotted to the next agency for yet another rejection.

Promoting a burger shop was a bit of a low point – the pictures landed in all the tabloids. Don't get me wrong: I like a burger, but sticking your head inside a giant burger to promote a new restaurant is a strange way to work as a model. The thing is, I wasn't just any type of model, I was an *Irish* model. Jobs like that were our bread and butter and at times I found myself jealous of the other models when someone landed an Eddie Rockets campaign – I bet those bitches got free wings or a gift card, the rage! It was a strange time in Ireland; those jobs were non-stop – they were called press calls and you got 100 euros to do them, although I was commanding 150 euros towards the end of my career, which was great for a couple of hours' work. Brands loved them, they got into the papers and because they didn't cost a huge amount of money everyone was at it.

The National Lottery once had me out in the snow on Dublin's Luas tram line in a bikini and heels (the usual uniform), holding a cardboard cut-out of the money that was up for grabs. I don't know if it generated any more Lotto sales but I do know it didn't make me want to buy a ticket (probably couldn't afford it anyway!). Shopping centre fashion shows were another big source of income and in fairness to Derek, my agent at the time, he created these shows so we could all make money. There would be a few shows a day modelling looks from each shop. Another 'modelling' job I had was at these big lunches full of wealthy women; we'd twirl around the tables in different outfits while they decided what they would buy. It didn't feel like real modelling then and it probably wasn't. Wedding fairs were another regular gig. We would model the dresses for potential brides and it's probably where my love of weddings comes from because I couldn't get enough of those dresses. At one of these shows I had 'forgotten' to go to sleep the night before (as in, I stayed up drinking until 6.30 a.m.) and headed straight to work. All that day I was giving sweaty bridal chic. It was very unprofessional of me but I'm pleased to say that it was the only time in my life I turned up to work drunk and I got away with it because they don't ask you anything at these events. Your silence is valued.

At the time I thought I was the bee's knees. But no matter how mortifying the 'modelling' was, I was never under any illusions. I knew that within the realms of modelling my level was Dublin, rather than Milan or New York, but I still wanted to get to the top of the game in my little patch, which I did. I worked a lot, made sure I did the best job I could with the hair that I had and was always rebooked. Modelling around the place was fun and I met some lovely girls along the way but the catwalks of Milan were safe from me.

There have been a few occasions in my twenties where I did think I was dying of a hangover and had to get the doctor over – I couldn't fly home from Asia once the hangover was so bad. My drink was vodka and Diet Coke and to this day I blame the hangovers on the ten Diet Cokes and not the ten vodkas. We always used to pre drink because we didn't have any money, but I could never get the balance right. I would drink a shoulder (500ml to anyone outside of Ireland) of vodka and two cans of Bulmers cider so by the time I got to the pub I had about an hour before my legs would start to go and I'd have to call it a night. My boyfriend would get so fucked off at me for it and rightly so because we would have to go home and miss a great night out.

Oh God, I've just remembered an awful habit of mine! In clubs I used to take small naps like a baby – off I would go into the toilet and lock the door, making sure to set my phone alarm to wake me. These are the times I would suggest taking yourself home, but because I was so terrified of missing any fun I would rather power nap on a toilet. One time the disabled toilet was free so I popped in there as it was very spacious and I conked out immediately, only waking up to bouncers banging on the door long after the club had closed. My panicked boyfriend had been looking everywhere for me. (If he knew me at all he would have known exactly where to find me.) I was in the dog box for that one for a while. How the night-clubs ever let me back in is beyond me.

Another time I decided to take the soap dispenser home with me from the same club – thanks for having me, CrawDaddy!* Of course when you're hammered you think this is gas craic, but what a wanker move for the venue. I did get soap all over my bag so I guess they got their own back. Eventually after all this messing around and being far too drunk an idea came to me: I would sneak the vodka in my bag into the pub and only drink the Bulmers in advance – genius! I would arrive at the pub pretty much sober and only order Diet Cokes all night, then leave falling around drunk. What a gobshite. When we went to the Trinity (University) Ball one year they were adamant nobody was sneaking drinks or drugs in and they checked everyone's coats and bags. Because I'm massively tall and dresses are mostly made for girls of a normal height my dress was tiny, which was okay with me (I kinda like the slutty lewk), but it didn't leave much room to hide any vodka. Didn't stop me though; I sellotaped a naggin of vodka to the inside top of my leg, saved myself a fortune and had a fantastic night.

It was around this time (the mid noughties) that I first started DJing. I had made some new 'town friends' (the

* A club in Dublin, now permanently closed.

town being Dublin City) including James O'Neill. James was and still is one of my wilder friends: when we go out, we go OUT! We used to party all weekend long and go back to the pub in the same clothes we had worn out the night before, scaldy little smelly things we were, but it wasn't really our fault because it was back when yokes were a fiver. God we had fun. (I fancy the pants off his husband Bryan but everyone does and he's cool with it.) When I'm in James's company I'm permanently smiling, everything is fun; but he is also great if you're going through a bad patch, the perfect ear to rant in. I will say though – and I'm quite sure James won't mind me saying this and if he does, he can't sue me because it's true – he is a desperate secret keeper. Full transparency here, I am too (I'm so bad that I tell the people who have made me swear not to repeat a secret that I probably will) but GOOD GOD if I killed someone, I wouldn't be telling James. I'd be locked up before the sun had set.

So while I'm waltzing around wedding fairs trying to make a living, one of our friends was running a club night called Can't DJ Won't DJ, where they invited pals to play ten songs each. A large part of my social life was going to see DJs in clubs and I've always been a huge music fan so I jumped at the chance. After that night I started taking it more seriously and would spend hours getting all of my music together, downloading songs and writing up my set lists. Recently, I found all my DJ cases and I just couldn't throw them out. There's some serious bangers in there. Because I couldn't live on my modelling income, I needed to have my fingers in as many pies as I could and DJing suited me down to the ground. At parties I was always getting in trouble for playing the music I wanted to and now I could play whatever I wanted and get paid for it! I even played the Trinity Ball once, no need to sneak vodka in that time! Booka Shade were headlining and I'm a huge fan of theirs. We had to do a little change over and I will never forget their faces watching in horror as I faded out one song to play the next instead of mixing, because I didn't know how to do it back then. A few lessons later and I was mixing away and playing different clubs.

One night a very famous DJ came into a club I was DJing at and played a few songs after me. There was talk of a party back at his hotel after the gig, but when I got into a car with him I soon realised nobody else was going to the party so I had a little freak-out and made him drop me back at the club. Sometimes I rage at my own frigidness because he was such a ride and I missed an opportunity to ride a ride. But I'd probably do the same thing all over again because I AM A FRIGID! Through DJing I got my first manager; he was a friend of mine who worked for MCD, a tour promoter in Ireland who later toured the live shows of *My Therapist Ghosted Me* – that felt like a full-circle moment. He got me really good gigs – gigs I didn't deserve at the time but I loved it. DJing in clubs is great fun. It's good to have technique and all that but I still think music selection is the biggest part of DJing. With the right tunes you could almost get away with not being able to mix, and if you're dying on your ass you just play 'Freed from Desire'. Everyone will rise!

My first foot in the TV door was when I got asked to do a reality type show called *Fade Street*. Originally it was about really rich girls from south County Dublin living their lives, but then the recession happened and you no longer needed to be from a really rich family on the southside of Dublin to be considered. There has always been a divide between the north and the south of Dublin. If you're a Southsider you are seen as posh and loaded although there are plenty of posh, loaded people on the north side too. It makes no sense but I don't make the rules! I was thrilled to get cast. At the time it was the biggest thing that had ever happened in my career and the 50 euro I was paid a day for filming 12-hour plus days seemed fair enough – I probably would have done it for free if I'd had to. That's the thing about the industry I'm in: you have to do a lot of stuff for free (I still do) but it usually leads to bigger paid jobs.

For the filming the producers set us up with 'jobs'. I was 'working' in a magazine for a period of time. That period was probably two hours total because I had real jobs and couldn't afford to give a pretend one much more time than that. The cameras would then follow me to my real gigs where I was DJing or 'modelling'. Because I was on TV it kind of felt like I was on the right path. Three of the girls on the show lived in an apartment on Fade Street, but I was living with my boyfriend so I stayed where I was. We moved in together quite early on because I had been kicked out of my house (again) and had nowhere to go. We shared a single bed in his place and because he was over six foot and I am a giant it was endless spooning so we could fit in the bed. I'm happy to say I was finally the baby spoon. At one point he told me how he would propose, in the tulip fields in Amsterdam. Tulips are my favourite flower and I thought that was very romantic.

The Fade Street girls hated living together and fought all the time. Like most reality shows the producers tried to pit us all against each other. One girl was the Spencer of the show and was always in trouble with someone. The producers really wanted me and her to clash, but it just didn't work. Not that I shy away from arguments or confrontation – I'm more than happy to stand up for what I think is right – but I don't like fighting with people I don't really know on camera. Overall, though, our show felt less nasty than the show Spen was a part of, which I genuinely think had no regard for the cast and how things might make them feel. On Fade Street I worked with producers that I would still work with today and I feel like I had a lucky escape in that sense. Nobody was out to try and ruin my life for the purpose of TV.

Chapter Nine

The Hardest Goodbye

While we were making *Fade Street* my dad's health was in rapid decline. Only a few years previously he'd had his first stroke and when Amber and I visited him in hospital it was distressing for both him and us. He had lost the use of his left side and couldn't speak properly, which had happened to his own father years before. It was awful; this was not a man willing to live like that, he would rather not live at all (at least that's what he said, but truthfully when faced with death, I'm not sure how you would decide that). When we left the hospital Amber and I were very upset for him and unsure of what we could do to help. All we knew was that our life and soul of the party dad couldn't survive the way he was. Miraculously, when we next went back in it was like he had reversed. His speech was back and he was able to walk; it was brilliant, but I still took it in my stride because there was the worry of whatever was coming next.

That next thing was his leg – it got so swollen that he had an open wound from his knee to his ankle. He didn't find it too hard to act normal (being around his leg as much as he was), but for us the sight of it was terrifying. He recovered from that but it wasn't long until it flared back up and he needed an operation, which meant there was a chance he would lose his leg, which he didn't want. For some reason I was the person who the hospital were going to call if a decision had to be made; maybe other people were on the list, but I knew I was to expect a call. This will sound very strange but Amber and I were at a festival the day my dad had the operation and I know this because I remember us celebrating and jumping around outside one of the tents when we got the call that my dad's leg was going to be saved. My dad was sick so often that our lives just went on, wrapped around his many operations and hospitalisations.

When I was filming *Fade Street*, he had quite a bad aneurysm in his stomach, the kind that if left alone would burst and cause a very painful death. This was terrible news. We were taken in to speak to his surgeon and told his chances of surviving weren't very good but that he wouldn't survive without the operation so he had no choice really. As was typical my dad didn't want to have the operation – he must have been very scared, but we all pushed him to have it because that was the best option. Regardless of that I still feel very guilty even now for it. He might have had an extra year, who knows. Initially it was good news: he had survived the operation and was recovering well so I went in to see him. It was only when I got there that I thought he didn't seem himself. He was saying things to me that he wouldn't usually say and I mentioned to the nurses that he didn't seem right.

Knowing he was in a bad way and he might not make it, I was filming a scene later that day in a bit of a dream state, just wanting to get the work done so I could go home. One of the cast was late and when she eventually did show up, spent the first ten minutes fuming that she'd had to walk there in the rain. 'Oh, sorry about your dad,' was all she said to me and then launched straight back to complaining. To this day I think that was weird behaviour and probably the worst part of the experience was pretending to be friends with people I didn't know that well when I was going through a tough time. Although they were all nice people we weren't really friends.

It's a bit of a blur from then on, but it transpired that my dad had had another stroke, this time affecting his brain. He was placed in an induced coma and brought to intensive care. He was there for a while – comfortable but not awake or responsive – and then his kidneys started to fail so we all knew there wasn't much that could be done. His body had given up the fight, but how lucky he was to have had as long as he did under the circumstances of a very, very indulgent and enjoyable life! He was moved into a private room and we all got to spend time with him before his life support was turned off; even then, he stuck around for another day. When he died he was surrounded by family and everyone he loved so at least he had that. It's the way I would like to go when that day comes.

He died in the Mater hospital in Dublin. He was so fed up with hospitals by the end of his life, although he had all of us holding his hands and helping him along. I think death is the scariest thing we will ever face and I always think when people die 'they did it', like it's some massive achievement, which it kind of is. I don't know if you've ever watched someone die but it's pretty wild. If you ever hear the death rattle, you'll know what it is.

My dad died of fun because he was always out drinking and smoking, having the absolute time of his life with zero concern for his health. It wasn't a surprise to any of us and I'm sure if there is an afterlife he would have been pretty chuffed with getting as far as he did living the life that he led, but it's still a ball of shit to lose a parent and it happens to all of us.

Freddie died around 6 a.m. on a Friday morning, which was very kind of him because everyone in Ireland knows a funeral is much like a party, a real celebration of that person's life and his would now be at the weekend (people get buried a lot quicker in Ireland than they do in Britain). It was actually the first night *Fade Street* aired so the joke in my family is that he died because he was so embarrassed for me. *Fade Street* quickly became the show that people loved to hate and if I wasn't on it I would have been slagging everyone else for being on it too!

First he went to my Aunt Sharon's house for his removal (night before funeral) and stayed in a single bed off the main kitchen and living room so people could pay their respects, as you do. My aunty's house is huge with big open spaces and a stunning Hamptons feel to the interiors, all pale blues and whites. The food, as always, was amazing so as far as wakes go it was a good one. Dad had a lot of good people around him so I do feel comforted knowing that he enjoyed his life, but I reckon most people would take more time if they could. I spent the removal dragging all my friends in to view him and say goodbye, much to their horror. A lot of people would rather not see a dead body but NOT ON MY WATCH! While I really wanted people to get to say a proper goodbye to him, as I've gotten older I realise that seeing someone in that way can be more disturbing than a way to get closure on their death. My Aunty Naomi has said she strictly wants a closed coffin and as Amber is the executor to her will, I won't even get to see the bod.

My pal Ashley was there on the day I decided he wasn't looking great (being dead and all) and tried to get her to touch up his make-up. Ashely insisted he was looking very well and my cousin Rebecca ended up doing it later on: *Bit of a red lip for the grave there, Freddie – don't you look absolutely gorgeous?* My poor dog Rocco got knocked over by a car outside my aunty's house that day. We were all quite distracted and he got out of the house. Thankfully he was grand but it wasn't the greatest timing. He used to dig up my dad's beloved garden all the time so maybe Freddie was getting him back from above. I'm joking, he loved dogs and Rocco was a belter even if he did help himself to my dad's hanging baskets whenever possible.

The night before his funeral Amber and I stayed up drinking beside him and chatting about his life. We decided we should stay in the room on the three-seater couch so he wasn't on his own. Waking up with a violent headache at 3 a.m. next to a dead body is not the most enjoyable thing so we quickly scampered off to our rooms (where we should have been in the first place) but it was a nice thought anyway! We buried my dad with 20 euros (for pints) and a pack of 20 Benson & Hedges because we are sound and knew he would need the basics as soon as he arrived upstairs. His funeral in all fairness was a hit, he got one he would have enjoyed attending himself, which he kinda did. He was just a little quiet.

I like to try and make light of every situation I can so I guess making jokes around my dad's death is my way of dealing with things, but losing him in my twenties was very difficult. As I write this his anniversary is coming up, fourteen years without him. When my Aunty Sharon sent me pictures of him to mark the occasion, I found myself wailing in the kitchen, which doesn't happen often but I just had such a wave of sadness for him – and for me if I'm honest. (I was sorting out the dog's dinner at the time, which totally reeks so that might have added to my sadness.) Shazzer always sends the most rotten pictures of my dad; she has one in her kitchen and his eyes look as though he's been up for three days but Sharon does have a knack for finding the worst pictures of him. She also called her French Bulldog 'Freddie' in his memory, which would have had him turning in his grave!

When you lose anyone, whether it be through a break-up or the more final end of death, it's tough. There isn't much you can say to someone besides the fact that you are sorry and thinking of them, which feels so pointless at the time. Like any kind of heartbreak grief needs time; in a way it is like heartbreak, just the worst kind and not the kind you can get over. You never think you'll get over a break-up, but you do eventually and then constantly remind yourself of what a geebag they were but the permanent loss of someone you love never goes away. I still think about my dad often. My dad always had my back, and until his untimely death at the age of sixty-eight, we had the greatest and best of times.

My boyfriend at the time was very kind. He took Amber and me shopping to buy us new black coats for the funeral but by then our six-year up/down, on/off relationship was coming to an end. It's crazy to think that you can love someone so much during a period in your life and then it all just disappears. Within six months I had broken up with him, met someone new and run away to Australia ... PHEW! We even got married. I make jokes about this all the time, but I have to make something funny out of something that definitely wasn't in hindsight. Very, very unlike me to do something so drastic but I put it all down to grief. I saw an opportunity to run from the sadness – and I took it.

Chapter Ten

Legged It

After *Fade Street* and the weird 'I hate it' success it received, I started to get more jobs, which meant that, despite what anyone thought about it, it had worked. Later *Fade Street* went onto make a second series and I made a deal to be in just part of one episode. As the years went by the show gained an almost cult following. Not to get ahead of myself – I don't mean a cult following like *The Goonies* or anything, but it has its own appeal; people in Ireland find it so ridiculous and still just love to hate it. It would seem it's the show that keeps on giving and good old RTÉ (Ireland's BBC) absolutely love to bring it back out on the RTÉ Player every so often, usually around Christmas, like a small gift to the nation and a giant lump of coal to me. My favourite thing about it is the dubbed versions that you find on YouTube; whoever did them I truly hope they are working in TV now, very talented. In most of the clips I walk into a room and as soon as I open my mouth the manliest sound comes out of it. Gas.

You'll have realised by now that I have never taken myself too seriously. I have done plenty of embarrassing things along the way, but I was young and having a lot of fun. I've never felt like I have to act a certain way or hang out with people that are deemed cool, I'm just happy in my spot. My approach is to have fun and avoid assholes. Very early on in my career, while I was on *Fade Street*, I was asked to film a skit, a funny video, with two guys who shall remain nameless. They had asked me to be a part of it or their management had, I'm not sure who. To get to the shoot I had to drive to the other side of the city at a time when I had zero cash so petrol money and parking was an expense I couldn't really afford. Still, I thought it would be a fun thing to do, even if I wasn't being paid.

When I got into the house they were filming in it felt weird straight away. Not the house itself but the vibe. By total coincidence I knew the house well as one of my pals lived there and to me it was one of the coolest places on earth, a place I could only dream of living in. It was a four-storey Georgian house just outside Dublin city centre that had been renovated with glass doors opening out to a beautiful garden. The two lads were nowhere to be seen and I was left downstairs for about an hour until their management came in and told me they wouldn't be filming with me. The lads, hiding upstairs, didn't have the decency to tell me themselves – I actually couldn't believe it. It turned out they didn't like the idea of filming with someone from *Fade Street*. Shame they didn't think of that before asking me to do the job and making me go the whole way over there. That day, even though I was really upset, I learned a valuable lesson: some people are so desperate to be seen as cool, that nothing else matters to them, not even common courtesy. Although I left feeling embarrassed, I soon came to the conclusion that they were the real idiots. Their duo has since broken up and one of them still works in the industry, but I will never see him as cool because I've seen this behaviour with so many people; they get a god complex because of what they do and it is the ultimate ick.

After *Fade Street*, Bill Malone at RTÉ offered me a job visiting the set of *Home and Away*. If you haven't watched *Home and Away* it's an Australian soap and a lot of its stars have become huge actors; it's a cesspit of Hollywood A-listers (think Chris Hemsworth, Heath Ledger and Isla Fisher). I realise how insane this might sound but MY GOD we love *Home and Away* in Ireland. With the gorgeous people and beaches, it's very similar to Ireland, just with endless sunshine rather than permanent rain. That's the main reason we like it so much I think, it reminds us of home in some kind of way. Off I went to meet its most famous residents, Alf and Irene, down in Summer Bay. I also had the time of my life in Sydney, meeting my old pals (lol, pal – I had one friend there). Ever since that first experience, travelling for free for work will never, ever lose its shine to me. Well, maybe if I was flying as much as Taylor Swift is. Actually no; I'd love that because I'd be on my own stunning private jet.

Recently I got offered a job and even though the money wasn't amazing, once they mentioned business class flights I almost passed away with excitement. Then I did pass away when my manager couldn't make the dates work. I love travelling and being able to see different cultures and amazing places around the world and I hope I never lose that because my mom flat out refuses to travel further than Spain, Dublin or London. We have booked Madrid for a girls' trip and even that was a push. 'Would we not go to Sotogrande?' No, Sandra, that's where you live, that's not broadening anyone's horizons.

After the success of the *Home and Away* special, RTÉ offered me my own documentary series, so off I went to interview the youngest woman on Death Row in America. I also spent some time in a military-style camp where underagers are sent before they end up in prison. What first struck me when we arrived was how clean and warm it was; I hadn't expected it to feel as hospitable as it did. There were classrooms and the place was run with military precision; in fact, it's exactly how I would like my home to be run. (Maybe I should adopt a more militant style of parenting and my floors would be forever gleaming?) All was going well until I got screeched at by prison guards to the point I was on the cusp of tears and had to ask my director to tell them to stop. It's a very strange thing having someone you don't know screaming in your face for looking at the ground, but that's how they do it in the States. If you rob a car, you could be facing twenty years in a privatised prison where the last thing they want to do is let you out because then how could they possibly make money? (That's the most political I'll get in this book, I promise.)

Things progressed for me in Ireland and I was getting on TV a lot more, which is no easy task and one I am still attempting to do. I love making all kinds of TV, whether it's live shows or documentaries – it's just something I can't shake. I filmed two more documentary series for RTÉ on different topics, but when Bill left RTÉ I could feel the nudge myself and knew I wouldn't be getting any more commissions. It was around this time I met my soon-to-be husband (too bloody soon). In fact possibly years too soon, because how ready is anyone to get married at twenty-six? We met on a night out after a TV show I was filming. One of the 'talent' (what anyone in front of the camera is called, even if they have no talent whatsoever) was being a creep and giving me attention I didn't want. At one point, when I was ordering a drink from the bar, he undid my bra strap, which really pissed me off. As well as being extremely immature and rude it was also very inconvenient; I can't put my bra on unless I turn it around at my tummy and clasp it that way. Along came my knight in shining armour and we just hit it off. He was fun and he took my mind off all the crap that was going on in my life.

We dated for the summer and then in a totally are-you-out-of-your-mind moment I did something that I would NEVER have done usually. I packed up my stuff and moved to Australia with him. I needed to get away from the sadness in Dublin and this felt like an adventure. Because I left Ireland quite hastily I had to pull out of a big TV show with RTÉ. The producer was raging and told me I'd never work for RTÉ ever again, which at the time scared the shite out of me, but we have laughed about it since. Both of us were equally pissed off with each other at the time and although I can be quite the fan of a good grudge, I let it go.

Everything we did together moved way too fast and to this day I don't know if that's because of what was going on in my life or if he was driving it forward. I missed home so much but luckily my pal Lynn moved over so I had her. As she wasn't loving her time there either, many a day was spent walking from Bondi to Coogee, thinking of how we could get back to Ireland. I also met another pal called James who is hilarious and just really good fun; a serial tanner at the time, when we went to the beach he had an app that would tell him to turn over in the sun. In those days I was still burning the life out of myself in the sun too, with not a thought to the damage to my skin. Whenever I see the sun now I feel like I'm melting and run for cover.

Australia was great for DJ gigs, but I still really wanted to work in TV. I did get some TV work while I was there, but the jobs were more about profile than money. Looking back, everything we did revolved around my husband, and I didn't put myself first very often; I was living his life, not my own and because of that it was easier to slot in with his social life. A few of his friends I really liked, but most of them were too old to be partying the way they did and had egos that weren't warranted. They thought they were brilliant and went out with women young enough to be their daughters (all over eighteen but still, some of his pals were in their fifties).

Some job opportunities did come through over there, which was great. I love being busy, but my career always felt less important than his – his career was much bigger than mine and at the time he earned a lot more money and was very generous with it. The problem is I'm not suited to following someone else around while they work, it's not the life for me. My previous relationship had been similar but this kind of dynamic could never last long because my career – no matter how small at the time – was important to me.

Living in Australia didn't suit me and I started to hate it there. A couple of years ago when I went back there on tour, I felt really sad because I realised Australia wasn't the problem at all – it's fantastic. It was who I was with that made me not want to be there. At the time I didn't have any really close friends and I wish I'd made more of an effort to get out and make some friends and create my own life. It really is an incredible country. They truly make the best coffee in the world, why can't we have the coffee beans they have? What are they doing differently? (I wouldn't take my word on that, though, because I only started drinking coffee a couple of years ago. Being absolutely shattered with a newborn drove me to coffee. I used to hate drinking it and would knock back a double espresso and nearly throw up straight after because it tasted like poison to me. As soon as I added milk I was grand; now I find myself telling people where to get a good coffee: Butlers, Dublin Airport – I'll have the free love heart chocolate, please!)

Eventually, I found a manager in Australia and got cast on *Dancing with the Stars*, which was a miracle in itself because of my two left feet and the fact that I couldn't have been less of a star, certainly over there! I grabbed the opportunity with both hands – something I always think you should do if it's a good one – and even though I had the grace of an elephant on the dance floor, somehow I didn't get the boot until week four. When you leave that show you're booked onto morning TV to discuss your eviction for being shite at dancing. Unfortunately, I had other plans and went on the absolute piss until 5 a.m. so I was in no fit state to talk to anyone at 7 a.m. Can you imagine my excuse? 'Sorry I'm very unwell. No, no I wasn't drinking!' (Bloody Pinocchio!)

My mom was so disappointed in me when she found out because the news went everywhere and she thought I was reinforcing the stereotype that all Irish people are pissheads. It was all over the papers and online at home, certainly not great for the résumé. 'Vogue Williams Too Hungover to Appear on Morning Television'. Scarlet! It was the only time I have ever called into work sick in my time in this industry. (I was always doing it when I was in college though, obviously.) Well, actually, I was covering my pal Ryan Tubridy's radio show in London last year and I did have to call in sick because I lost my voice. There he was wishing me luck on my first day!

Recently, years after that experience, I got offered the *Strictly* Christmas special, and even though my dancing is awful, I thought why not? It didn't happen for me in Australia but surely *someone* could teach me to dance? Much to the disappointment of my dance teacher and the production staff I simply couldn't get it; they had assumed I could dance because I work out – big mistake, my friends. The professional dancer I was paired with, Carlos, thought I'd be able to dance because according to him I look like a dancer. Poor Carlos got the fright of his life when I did my first move. He also kept telling me how he was going to teach me to walk like a woman, which gave me a great laugh; the old 'wide gait' strikes again. Eventually I broke Carlos and got a new dance partner, Gorka, a very good dancer but half my height. I went around the dance floor like Lurch from *The Addams Family*. While I'm still not a natural dancer I did notice one massive difference in myself all these years later: I felt so much less stressed second time around. These days I have much more of a 'fuck it' attitude. You don't have to be brilliant at everything but I wanted to try give it my best shot. Yes, it still wasn't good enough, but I had a lot of fun.

Chapter Eleven

BIG WEDDING,
small marriage

When we got engaged I was embarrassed to ring my family and tell them because I knew they would think it was wrong; in all honesty it didn't feel to me like the right thing to do either. Also, I knew they would try to hide their actual feelings and put on a mask of happiness so as to not hurt me or cause an argument (knowing I might never speak to them again, what with me and my holding grudges. All childish and immature of course but I was both of those things at the time). This was the only time in my life that I really felt a distance from Amber; as well as the physical distance, she wasn't very keen on how fast things were moving. We did drift slightly during that time but I can't see it ever happening to us again.

I did assume that we'd have a long engagement – that's what I wanted so I could enjoy it – but he wanted to get married as soon as possible.

The first wedding I ever went to was my Aunty Sabina's. The mad yoke invited the kids along, me included, even though I was very young. What stuck out most to me from that wedding was the adult men weeing outside, a whole row of them. I was fascinated by this and convinced if I looked hard enough I might spot a penis, but sadly that wasn't to be. Of all my pals, I was the first to get married – no wonder considering, at twenty-six, we were barely out of the womb. In my mind I wanted the big white fairytale wedding and it all started with the dress. In Australia the designers J'Aton had the most incredible wedding dresses and agreed to design one for me.

There were two big magazine deals in place; we didn't have a huge income at that time although it probably looked like we did, but our cars were leased and houses were rented. Having someone pay for the wedding seemed like an easy decision and I don't regret it, even today; you get your hair, make-up and styling done and the magazines take the best pictures. The wedding was in a gorgeous castle in Florence, the food was amazing, the cake was amazing and the flowers were stunning and ridiculously expensive. On paper it was the wedding of dreams. The only problem was that I wasn't the happiest bride because it was the wrong decision and the wedding was a fucking NIGHTMARE. We had done the registry office bit in a total blur and were officially married before we even touched down to our wedding party in Italy. On the night we arrived, my parents were meeting his parents for the first time in a restaurant. Clearly, it was unusual that our parents had never met before. At the time I blamed it on us having been in Australia but I reckon both sides thought this union was a bad idea from the get-go. That night I got completely hammered, for which I blamed Italian measures. My mom had to tell him to bring me home.

Absolutely deranged, I almost fell down the stairs in the restaurant. On the walk home I threw my shoes at him in an argument and he threw them into the river. He was right to do that but if I'm being very picky, he did litter. Litterbug. We were still arguing when we got back to the hotel and that's when I decided it would be a great idea to throw our rings off the balcony. Luckily they got stuck in a tile and were easily retrieved. Still deranged, I slipped on one of my bags and whacked my face on the floor but, fortunately, my wrists caught most of the force. That was the last thing I remember before I woke up the next day – the day before our wedding.

Opening my eyes to a pounding headache and a strange feeling in my face and my lips, it all came back to me in a rush. I jumped out of bed and looked in the mirror to be greeted with a totally bruised chin and a massively swollen lower lip; the kind of lip someone would pay for minus the bruising. Ashley was doing my make-up for the wedding and came straight up to the room to assess the damage: it didn't look good but she assured me some tattoo make-up from MAC would do the job. She has since told me that she felt like crying because it was so bad; not only did she feel really sorry for me, but this was also a really big job for her as two very big magazines were showcasing her work. I felt so stupid and guilty about the whole thing.

The morning of the wedding I felt very stressed and so anxious because deep down I knew I had made a mistake. He probably felt the same, I'm not really sure. It was supposed to be the happiest time of our lives and it really wasn't. His best man didn't even show up to the wedding, can you imagine? He'd actually flown the whole way to Italy from Australia, made a big deal on his huge radio show about the wedding and then sacked it off in favour of going on a bender not too far from where the wedding was on.

After the wedding I tried to make things work, tried to make our place in London a home and made up a bedroom for his kids so they could come and visit. We had moved into an apartment of his but it had taken us a long time to get the woman who was renting it out; she hadn't paid rent in over a year and generosity to a complete stranger can only last so long, especially when you have nowhere to live until she leaves. We were very accommodating but she was furious. When we eventually got the keys and walked in the place smelled unbelievably bad, like the worst smell you can imagine. In a rage she had decided to put all her pots on the hobs in the kitchen and boil shit. She had boiled faeces on the hob and the stench was horrendous. It was almost impossible to get rid of it, even with a full paint job. I used those Glade plug-ins everywhere and still I can't bear the smell of them, it just reminds me of that awful time.

When we moved back from Australia to Ireland and then onto London, I felt so much happier to be back around my family and friends. I'd only been away eighteen months but I'm a big baby and I missed my mom. I also brought my pooch Winston back, one of the loves of my life. I got Winston as a puppy in Australia and when we were moving back so many people wanted to keep him as they didn't think we would fly him home but I was going nowhere without him. Winston was the only argument in our eventual divorce proceedings: we both wanted him, but I knew I would take better care of him. Eventually we settled on joint custody, which was never going to work. I knew it wasn't fair on him and after many missed turns of my ex taking Winston, I decided I was keeping him. I'm glad to say he still lives very happily with me now and costs me a fortune in vet bills!

The relationship wasn't all terrible, we did have some great times too and for the most part he was good fun to be around, but he was not husband material. It was me who called it in the end. I couldn't keep trying, it felt pointless. Like I said at the start, I'm not here to throw anyone under the bus but there are things that went on in our relationship that will never be forgiven. I've moved on, of course, but I found things out after we had broken up that I wish I'd known earlier; things that if I had known, the relationship would have been over long before we ever got married.

Missteps are a part of life and I try not to regret mine too much as they have all led me to where I am now. But there is one thing I do feel so angry with myself over: that I gave away that wedding dress from J'Aton. At the time I didn't have the room to store it AND my Christmas tree, and as I viewed the dress as a bad omen I gave it away in a moment of rage. How I wish I had kept that dress. It was glorious, like a stunning, giant ice cream; I have yet to see a wedding dress that was nicer than it. Sometimes I'll daydream about where she went to and who wore her ... On the plus side I really love my tree, it's pre-lit and very realistic-looking.

It was such a relief when we decided to get a divorce, like a weight had been lifted from my shoulders. We continued living together for some time after; we didn't hate each other, we just knew we couldn't be together. We released a statement (cringe) and then it's all people wanted to know about. It was only after we got divorced that I questioned why he ever wanted to get married. Looking back at things I know now (but didn't then) it makes no sense that he was in such a hurry. Maybe because he had been married before and engaged before, he wanted to prove this one was going to work. Or maybe I'm being very unromantic (very possible) and he just really wanted to marry *me*? But in all honesty, I don't really think that was it.

I found my own place to live with a friend in London and it was pretty grim, but I didn't care because the main thing I wanted was to live with someone I knew. The thought of being lonely really scared me; I had been in long-term relationships since I was nineteen years old so it felt very weird. Now I was thirty and divorced, which I found mortifying. I had wanted to be married with kids at thirty, not divorced and single.

Chapter Twelve

Divorcée

After the breakdown of my marriage I became very anxious; I think it was the sheer embarrassment of the whole thing that gave me my first real wave of debilitating anxiety. It was the I-told-you-sos from everyone that really started working me up, but at the same time I was so relieved to be out of that marriage. It was a confusing time. This new level of anxiety was quite disastrous and it's probably what triggered my sleep obsession: a good night's sleep was what really went down the toilet. During the day I could handle feeling anxious because I could set myself the task of getting rid of it, which distracted me a little, but once it messed with my sleep I started to feel like I was losing control. Being woken up by a really fast heartbeat and pains in my stomach became a constant thing. One night I even took myself to a SwiftCare Clinic, convinced I was having a heart attack – with bad hearts running in my family, I thought it best to get it checked out. Turned out I was having my first panic attack, and what a joy it was – not! As a naturally happy and upbeat person, this new feeling of being in such a tizz was not really on brand for me. That night was the first time I realised that maybe I wasn't as well put together as I thought.

While I didn't have a panic attack until after my marriage ended, I think anxiety was always there in the background, just waiting for some traumatic event to turbo-charge it. All through my life I've been busy touching wood – no, not that kind of wood, please remove your mind from the gutter! I always touch wood in the hope that it will stop anything bad happening to me or someone close to me which, because I have an anxious mind, is something I worry about quite a lot. If I'm really stuck for a piece of wood to touch, I'll tap my head three times because someone told me it's the same thing and naturally I believed it as I do everything until I am proven wrong. I've even been known to throw in a few holy bits too, like praying to Saint Anthony should I ever lose something or begging God to find me a parking space in central London – which would be completely impossible without his help.

I'm surprised I never went down the white witch route or joined a cult because it would have been a logical step for me at one point of my life. All the usual things like never walking under ladders, crossing anyone on the stairs or smashing mirrors I'm careful about and I'd never put new shoes on the table. I feel bad about this, but when I'm buying shoes in Zara, I'll give them to the sales assistant to put on the table so I don't get the bad luck. Whenever I pass a graveyard, I bless myself twice as blessing yourself once you open up your intention and I don't need Him knowing what I get up to until I pass another graveyard. If He did, I doubt I'd ever make it through the pearly gates. (All this would suggest I believe in God, but it's more that I believe in a Higher Being that I call God, thanks to the Catholic Fear inflicted upon me as a child.)

There are so many different forms of anxiety. You've got your generalised anxiety disorder, panic disorder, social anxiety disorder, and various phobia-related disorders and then within them you have a load more. Each disorder causes different reactions in people so it's like a giant spider's web of panic. Back in the day, it was far simpler; they would just say that your nerves were at you. Now, I would diagnose myself with a touch of OCD (courtesy of my mother) with a sprinkle of intrusive thoughts and maybe a dash of THE FEAR. My mother is a neat FREAK. Sandra has a table of silver at her house in Dublin that she curses every time she goes home yet insists that she absolutely loves it. On every visit to Ireland she spends two hours polishing her silver and then gazes at it adoringly but hates it again when it inevitably loses its shine and the Silvo has to come back out. Still, she refuses to get rid of it. I'll tell you what, when she meets her maker that's the first thing I'll be getting rid of. By the way, I'm telling you this story to try and give you an insight into why I am so obsessed with cleaning, I didn't lick it off the ground!

Intrusive thoughts are probably the worst aspect of anxiety for me. When people tell me they meditate for forty minutes a day, I just think how is that possible? They just fall asleep and then call it meditation – it has to be that. If I closed my eyes and attempted meditation the only thing that would happen is I'd consider the many ways I might die or I'd stress out about the day I will find my twelve-year-old dog Winston dead in his basket. How would I deal with his remains? Living in London with no garden, I worry about that particular problem a lot. At the risk of sounding a bit cray, I have had many intrusive thoughts. I've read that they can range from mild to quite violent – mine are on the milder side so it's all good, but, if you find yourself sitting on the violent side of the fence and they are recurring, I think it may be an idea to get some help.

There's been times I have found myself literally shaking my head when I've come round from a trance that has brought me down the strangest path in my mind. For instance, if I were to close my eyes now the strangest scenarios would come into my head and scare the absolute shite out of me. One time I read a story of a young man who got very drunk on a night out and ended up falling asleep in a wheelie bin. It probably started out as a joke, but then he actually dozed off, was wheeled to the truck by the bin men, dropped into it and crushed to death in an instant. An awful story, but when I read that I had weeks of imagining myself meeting such a fate. I also have a lot of anxiety around death but, again, that's a whole other chapter of fun to get through.

Alcohol is definitely my main anxiety trigger, but I'm not ready to give that up for life just yet. Some people get beer fear whereas I get 'my life is over' fear, for absolutely no reason. My husband Spencer will always say: 'Why don't you just remember that it's down to drinking so forget about feeling like this?' If only it was that easy, my friend, now please excuse me while I catastrophise everything about my life for the rest of the day. When I'm hungover my anxiety is at peak levels, unless the hangover is so severe that my brain isn't working properly. This has only happened a few times in my life, but when I tell you six margaritas is too many margaritas please believe me. My head felt like it was being crushed in a vice and although sometimes a distraction from my anxiety is nice, nothing was worth that pain. What snake invented frozen margs? It's a sneaky little invention – so much alcohol that it will mess you right up but bizarrely delicious so you don't realise how drunk you are getting until it's too late. I don't know about you but drink four is the point of no return for me. The fear will hit me like a bus around four and a half hours after I've fallen asleep, jolting me right out of that glorious comatose state. The rest of the day is filled with self-hatred and my continuous questioning of why I have put myself in that position. How could I allow myself to feel this awful for six hours of fun?

Anyone with anxiety will have their different ways of coping with it. My way is to train, eat well, try to get a good night's sleep and avoid alcohol. Training I find incredibly helpful; a good workout can change my whole mindset for the day and I never regret a run or getting myself out for some kind of exercise. I also see a therapist, very irregularly. While I do enjoy therapy, it makes me feel a bit like I'm not allowing myself to cope on my own, that I'm not in control, but my therapist has told me I'm a control freak (in a much nicer way) so it all makes sense. Lastly, I have a stockpile of beta-blockers that block the release of the stress hormones adrenaline and noradrenaline in certain parts of the body. This results in a slowing of the heart rate and reduces the force at which blood is pumped around your body. In normal talk, they stop the physical symptoms of anxiety so you can deal with the root cause of it through therapy or, in my case, so I can stop grinding my teeth. There's nothing wrong with taking medication, but I'll usually try and wait until it's absolutely necessary.

Coming up to my thirtieth birthday, and with a few not-so great relationships under my belt, I decided to so some proper work with a therapist to figure out why I kept ending up in the same situation with men. For the briefest of moments I was even willing to blame myself, a completely ridiculous thought! I have always had strange taste in men – Eric Cantona, Liam Gallagher, all the bad boys. I also used to be completely mad about this guy who constantly had foam around the corners of his mouth – everyone in my friend group was repulsed, but evidently it was a real turn on for me. Especially when he would drink red wine and the colour would change … my God it really was gross.

Another guy I was with would literally snow on me – his dandruff was so intense that any movement would create a snowstorm. I did try everything to help him, but all of it made it worse (paracetamol crushed up in shampoo does not work). It's only when you come out of a relationship that you can look back and think good God, how did I put up with that? And then there's all the narcissists, the most heavily thrown around word on the internet. Isn't it interesting how our exes are all narcissists and anyone who crosses us shall be diagnosed as a narcissist immediately? I had a friend once who, whenever she broke up with someone, proclaimed that they were either gay, a narcissist or both. It is amazing what we will tell ourselves when we feel we've been disregarded. Can't be me, must be them!

In my first marriage there was a lot of partying and drinking going on and it's never good for any relationship. As I have a tendency to gravitate towards people who drink, this was always on the cards for me. My therapist once told me that children of alcoholics will find themselves around alcoholics and people who drink a lot in later life. Although I don't like calling my dad an alcoholic, he was certainly functioning that way for most of my life and the main way I know how it's affected me is that I've often ended up with people who are too 'fond of the drink'. We came to this conclusion – well, my therapist eventually had to tell me (after I had completely exhausted him) – that this was the overall issue. He had to spell it out because even though it was right in front of me, I couldn't see it.

I'm drawn to men with alcohol-related issues or bad depression and anxiety who need help, help I think I can give them. Thankfully, I've since figured out that it's impossible to help anyone who doesn't want to help themselves. Some people want to stay at that point in their life and not you nor anyone else can change that. It was a hard lesson to learn because it meant that many of my relationships had been doomed from the start; I could also see parallels with my professional life. There have been times I have been fucked over and then blamed myself for trusting certain people, which makes it even worse. It's natural to want to see the best in people and to be honest and I'll never change, but I've been burnt professionally a couple of times so I try to be more of a lone wolf these days.

Some of the relationships I needed to work through in therapy had involved ugly things like cheating and manipulation. One relationship I stayed in even though I knew I'd been cheated on; you have to take each situation on board and decide for yourself what you want, and if you think you can move on and forgive then that's up to you. Doesn't mean it doesn't hurt though. It's also a very hard thing to forget and those feelings will always arise so I'm not actually sure how people manage to get over it; in the end I wasn't able to. I'm loyal as a dog when it comes to friends and relationships and if it's not reciprocated, I just can't keep that person in my life. As much as I might try to move past it, the thought of how they hurt me will always linger in the back of my mind. Being manipulated by a partner is a really strange place to be in because it messes with your head so much and you're constantly questioning yourself. They make you think you're the problem and you're the one who's wrong and you start to believe it. You can lose yourself in a situation like that because they pick away at you until you barely know what's going on and just assume most things are your fault.

There was another relationship I stayed in much longer than I should have and when we broke up, I found out he had been serially cheating on me. I was lucky that I hadn't ended up at the doctors with some unwanted disease. It came to me in a few ways because there were quite a few people: one girl actually contacted me on Instagram to tell me she was in the middle of her ten-step programme and gave me all the details of what had happened between her and my ex, so it really was undeniable. I almost responded and then realised that her telling me was more for her benefit than mine so in the end I decided to ignore her message. I can be the bigger person in most circumstances but not in that one.

When you find out things like that about someone you really thought you knew it can make you feel like such an idiot. Being hurt romantically by anyone has to be one of the worst feelings in the world. There have been times I have been in physical pain when I have been heartbroken, hyperventilating from the amount of crying I did and I wouldn't wish that on my worst enemy. Since then I've realised that it's their shame not yours and it's important to hold your head up high. The thing about heartbreak and sadness is that you don't want to do anything except hide away, but if you can say yes to those invitations, just make yourself go even if you don't want to. Eventually you will start feeling better and your heart will mend too.

I've never been on a dating app – meeting people through Twitter is as close as I've gotten to one – but I reckon it would be quite fun. The only problem would be that I'd pick apart every single thing about someone. Oh, he has a weird-looking thumbnail. SWIPE. Ewwww, look at that freckle on his cheek. SWIPE. My moley moley would probably make a tonne of people swipe away too. One of my first dates after my divorce was very good-looking but my God he was loud – can you imagine how loud he was if I'm saying that? Another fella was sound and owned a cool company but I think he wanted more than I did. Also his toilet was very dirty and I hate myself for saying this, but as a self-confessed neat freak it was a red flag. Booze problem? All good. Dirty toilet? I'm sorry but no way. There were a few dates with a footballer but it was only ever for a bit of fun. I met him at an event and he DMed me on Twitter afterwards. When we started talking he was actually really sound and we got on very well, but ultimately he was not for me. Another guy was in the public eye and I had fancied him for years – not actively fancied him in a weirdo way, but if I saw him pop up on things I'd think, ride! We went out for a while, then he ghosted me. He sent me a text months later to see what I was up to – the cheek of him! At the time my self-confidence was in the toilet so I went running back as fast as my legs could carry me. Then he ghosted me again.

Next there was a gorgeous guy from Copenhagen that I dated for a while until he started saying weird stuff about my career. He would often ask me if the paps were outside the windows, which in a sense was flattering because the paps had very little interest in me at that time. (Their interest hasn't risen much and if I ever do see a pap outside my house, I immediately rack my brain to think of any possible mistake I've made as that's the only reason they could possibly be around.) He also made it very clear that he wasn't going to treat me in a particular sort of way because of what I did for a living and I found that really strange. This lad definitely had the wrong end of the stick: I think he thought he was dating Britney Spears when I was still at the backing dancer stage. Fame in that sense can be a weird thing, because although I'm slightly more well-known now and at times get recognised, I wouldn't ever think it could impact anyone's view of me ... but I guess it does with some people. Probably I do it too with people I view as famous; I do get a bit more nervous and unsure of what to say sometimes, but that's only with *really* famous people!

Then there was a strange phase of men wanting to take me on holiday after two dates. It sounds great. I mean who doesn't want a free holiday, but it's a bit full-on and it made me run. One night I bumped into a guy I had kissed at a members club and he was sitting with another guy my pals were trying to set me up with and who I'd been texting. I tried and failed to hide and the guy I was texting was so pissed off that that possibility went out the window. Then there was a small thing with a grime rapper I met online, but it never turned into anything more than a kiss. I feel like I did a lot of texting and kissing but not much else!

I really wanted to date and have fun being single for as long as I could, but soon I was seeing just one person (very me). I should have been single for longer but a relationship has the potential to kick you in the face sometimes and it's hard not to commit. It was all very full-on and he was (and still is) very intense and chaotic. He was a total whinger but I fancied him so I stuck around. There was always something wrong with him, some kind of illness that never was. I joke and say I whinge all the time, but I'm really quite a positive person and hanging out with a whinger rubs off on you. But he was hot so I let him get away with it. He's gone even more off the charts over the years and in fear of people thinking I have totally lost the plot I won't say his name. (That is unless I meet you out or something and I've had a drink, then I'll tell you and we can watch my birthing video straight after!) But MY GOD if I told you who he was I'd Never Live It Down! (Podcast plug!)

He used to have a full-time housekeeper, a nanny for his kids when they were over, an assistant, a life coach and a therapist. Oh AND a reiki guy. Imagine all that and you still can't keep your shit together? He also used to smoke rollies and he would smoke in the house, in bed, anywhere he wanted and leave a trail of destruction behind him; tobacco and skins just strewn all over the house, his cleaner had long given up trying to clean up all of that. He was the dirtiest smoker I have ever encountered, and that includes my dad who tipped his cigarette ash on the floor. He also insisted on falling asleep to Radio 4, which was annoying for someone like me who likes white noise or silence.

One time he tried to set up pap shots of us and succeeded – I looked like complete shite because I wasn't expecting it and had just come off the back of a two-day drinking extravaganza. Looking rotten was the least of my worries, though; I really didn't want to be photographed with him because it wasn't anything very serious. Although he denied setting it up, I know it was him because he constantly asked if we could set up shots at something wholesome like a Christmas market – can you imagine? I do a lot of mad things in my career but I don't set up pap shots. No shade to people who do that, but it's not my vibe.

(Top tip, if you want to know who is setting up their own pap shots it's anyone who gets papped in Dubai. It's illegal to be a pap there so they are all hired in.)

Chapter Thirteen

Love on the Slopes

My big break in the UK was on the TV show *Bear Grylls: Mission Survive*. Filming began when my brother was getting married so I had to miss that, but then again he missed my first wedding (although he did tell me he would go to the next one, which he did to be fair to him). At his wedding he had all of his groomsmen hold lightsabers (Frederick is a fun geek) so he and his wife could walk under them, which she did while hiding her face. I'm pretty sure that was the last time she ever let him choose anything and she's dead right. (I don't want to get him into trouble but he spent about four hundred quid on those lightsabers which makes it all the more embarrassing.) This year I got him in Secret Santa and he wanted a contribution to a Star Wars Lego yoke that costs £800 – I told him to get a grip. He has loads of Lego and hates when his son wants to play with it because he wrecks it.

On Bear *Grylls: Mission Survive* I drank my own piss, ate live scorpions and roasted rats on the fire – all in the name of TV! There wasn't much I wouldn't do to win that show and advance my career. Warm piss? YES PLEASE! I enjoyed the show; Bear Grylls is pretty sound and I made really good friends with Tom Rosenthal but some of them on that show were just ridiculous. I'm not here to name names but one person threw a filthy little strop for being thrown off the show, went back to the hotel and cleared out the entire mini bar in a fit of spite. GET A GRIP. At the end of the day I was willing to look semi-foolish if it meant progressing my career – how could I learn from anything if I didn't try stuff out? Maybe I do look back and feel that slight twinge of cringe (that rhymes … poetry book next), but I am at a point where I can laugh at all the ridiculous stuff I've done, professionally and personally, because it's brought me to where I am today.

With a lot of jobs I've done people have asked me why I was doing them – not in a curious, kind way but more of a 'What makes you think you can do that?' way. It started when I began working on a construction site. In the end I knew it wasn't for me, but it's not to say I wasn't capable of the job. The same when I was modelling, DJing, making TV documentaries in Ireland or trying to build a profile in the UK. Through it all my goal has always been focused in one direction: hosting a Saturday night, shiny floor TV show. Whatever it takes to get there – be it modelling wedding dresses, interviewing participants at an Irish orgy (more on that later) or doing my fair share of reality TV – I've been happy to do it. All of it, including *The Jump*, a ski show where 'celebs' compete against each other to jump the furthest. That's where I met my second husband. Enter Spencer.

Our first encounter was at the ski slopes of Hemel Hempstead. I knew Spencer was doing the show because a guy I was casually dating at the time told me he was. He also warned me about what a total wanker Spencer was, but as I like to form my own opinions on people I didn't take that on board, even though I did kind of think the same from seeing him on TV and reading about him in the papers (which was bad of me as it's all based on complete rubbish). It's not until you meet Spencer that you realise he's a very charming, funny, generous and kind person. A lot of people have opinions on Spen from when he was in his twenties on a constructed reality TV show, where he was paid more to play the villain, a role he took to like a duck to water (ever the professional, my Spenno). On that show he was doing what most of us did when we were younger; just on TV, instead of in private!

Technically, the ski slopes of Hemel Hempstead wasn't our first time meeting, though. Around three years earlier I was away on a work trip with a brand in Ibiza and on my way back up to my room I bumped into Spencer and his girlfriend at the time, who were staying in the same hotel. He didn't seem to be in very chatty form but I thought she was very nice. We chatted about the Bear Grylls show and she complimented me on my win so I immediately liked her. (A compliment goes a long way in my book.) They were going out for dinner that night with friends and they invited me to go with them, but I couldn't go because they were going to a ridiculously expensive place that cost 400 euro a head. I don't even think anywhere is worth that now and certainly not then.

Only after writing this do I wonder what would have happened if we had gotten to know each other that evening. I genuinely think we would have been friends (I would never have entertained anything else anyway, as he was in a relationship) and would have gotten along as well as we do now. But if he had been single and we'd connected, I don't think it would have gone very well because I get serious quickly without even meaning to and he had yet to form a serious bone in his body. Also, at the time, I was just out of my marriage and considering going out with someone I had already dated, as you do when you firmly believe you will die alone. Hanging on and trying again for old times' sake never works.

We did get on famously from the start of *The Jump*. He wandered in late, reeking of booze (tick tick for me) and wearing tracksuit bottoms and a pair of slippers that looked like he had stolen them from his dad. It was obvious he was intent on making a beeline for me but I wasn't going down that road. As discussed, I had done a lot of prior work with my therapist up to this point; we had decided that if I continued to fall for guys I felt I needed to fix or help I was just repeating a pattern and that it always ended the same way (disastrously). Spencer, being yet another man made out of red flags, was not for me I decided, and I didn't really fancy him anyway so it was all good. I did, however, love his personality. My friends were really excited he was on *The Jump* and really wanted me to sleep with 'Spencer Matthews', but I told them even though that wasn't on the cards he would definitely be a permanent member of our friendship group. (The main culprits trying to make me jump on Spencer Matthews were James and Bryan. They thought he was a ride and wanted to get all the details, which they did – in the end.)

As soon as we left our first ski session, Spencer was DMing me on Twitter suggesting we go for drinks, which I wasn't up for, but he settled for getting my number. Not long after he rang and asked me to go out with him and his friends, but I politely declined. It wasn't until we flew to Austria that we saw each other again. (I'd recently ended things with the whinger as he was looking for something more serious than I wanted.) A couple of nights into the trip and after about four vodkas Spencer and I kissed, but I really wanted to keep it a secret because

I didn't want it turning into anything serious. (Spencer, of course, didn't keep it secret yet I continued to deny.) In general, there was a fair bit of messing going on during filming; I guess things will happen when you throw a load of 'celebs' in a hotel with a bar.

While Spenny was drinking a lot and I couldn't (nor did I want to), I was texting a few other love interests, trying my best not to revert to Relationship Girl. Still, even though neither of us wanted a relationship at the time we kept ending up together. When my sister came to visit during filming I tried to deny the relationship, but as I was staying in his room while she was there so she and her partner could have my room, she knew something was going on. Before the competition started I snapped my anterior cruciate ligament (ACL) because I didn't clip my ski boot in properly. I was devastated because I really enjoyed that show; still, I had gotten to compete in all the events during training so it was worth it. They never quite managed to kill anyone off on *The Jump* but I know that one girl broke her neck. It was pretty wild, but then again, if you're flinging yourself off the side of a mountain what do you expect? When I signed I had a feeling something might happen to me because I had gotten away with very little bodily damage up to that point of my life and it felt like my turn.

Spen came into my hospital room unannounced (as usual) when I had just come round from the operation and been given an unusual amount of laxatives. For the previous hour before his arrival there was a serious hurricane blowing in that hospital room; it was like opening the door of a plane after a long-haul flight and just being battered with stink! I believe it went unnoticed, unless he was too polite to say. Things were still very casual between us and when I went home I did very well for myself – when I tell you a leg brace is like honey to a bee when it comes to men, you have to believe me. When we had parties in my house, I would very kindly invite any rides I was kissing back; clueless, they thought I was inviting them back for other reasons and then be disappointed when I didn't want to go to my room. Why the hell would we go there when a party was going on?

I'm never one to leave a good party. Sometimes I think I'd rather not go to a party at all because I find the leaving part so difficult. It's hard to say no to fun! Amber recently sent me a photograph of myself fast asleep on a couch at a party in her old one-bed apartment – there are people sitting around me smoking and drinking! They had tried to get me to go to bed, but I wouldn't, so they continued to party around me. It's a problem; when I drink I literally have to be forced to go to bed. It's why I drink so rarely now; I'd rather just be in my bed as early as possible because (if I haven't already mentioned) I love sleeping. Thinking about it, one of my favourite things about being in a relationship is that you always have someone to get you to bed! If it wasn't for Spen I would be up until 6 a.m. every time we go out and then cry about it for the entire week.

Spen is the nicest person in the world to be hungover and fear-y with. He will never ever tell you if you did anything embarrassing and will, at all costs, try to make you feel better. If I ever started renting him out for hangover days, I'm telling you, he'd be booked out. Imagine your pal calls you and says: 'I can't believe what you did last night!' That feeling that goes directly to the pit of your stomach is what medical professionals call anxiety. This would be a good time to rent Spencer. (By the way, if a friend ever did that to you my advice is to ditch them; you don't need that kind of negativity in your life. If they want to remind you of something your mind has kindly blocked out for you, get them out of your life.) One of the many reasons I love Spencer so much is that even during lockdown when I occasionally fell asleep on the couch after drinking with a couple of pals, he never mentioned it and I thought what a kind soul, you lovely, lovely man. Now hug me because I despise myself!

When Spenny finished *The Jump* (well, won *The Jump* – no surprise there), we decided to make it official and we were quick movers after that. Most of our free time we spent together and on weekends we were either drunk or lounging in bed hungover and eating endless takeaways. I would love to go back and do one of those weekends again where we had no responsibilities. We were disgusting: we'd just stay in his apartment and drink, watch TV and eat. It was rotten but also glorious. What I very quickly learned is that Spen has no boundaries at all. If you ever meet him you are guaranteed to feel like he is invading your personal space. He's a space invader!

At first when I stayed with him I would always go to the café across the road to use the toilet, if you catch my drift. He had an ensuite in his apartment and that was it; it also had this really light sliding door with zero soundproofing. One evening I was there and had to use the toilet and had no choice but to risk it. (By the way, I'm not completely insane: I would wee there, no problem, but we hadn't yet gotten to the other part of our relationship.) That evening I felt comfortable enough to take the big step, which was my first mistake, because within a second of sitting down on the toilet seat Spencer opened the door and weirdly just stood there talking to me about fruit while I died of embarrassment. How great the grapes at Marks & Spencer were at that time of year wasn't of a major concern to me right at that very moment. I mean, they were like apples and completely delicious, but there's a time and a place and that was neither of them.

I love describing people in three words: you have to be so careful what you choose as it's very limited. The three words I would pick to describe Spencer are eccentric, fun and generous. Spencer lives in his own universe; I've never met anyone quite like him and while we do have some qualities in common, he has qualities that I most definitely do not. First and foremost he is absolutely wild about himself. I admire it, but it's also crazy to be so happy with yourself. I have never met another soul who wouldn't change a single thing about themselves. Spen's mom, Jane, thinks I'm the same so I must be good at hiding my insecurities because that is not how I feel about myself! Trust me, I have a very long and ever-expanding list for self-improvement.

One of my absolute favourite things about Spen is his ability to order the most incredible spread at a restaurant – his ordering skills are next to none. We are like two dump trucks when we go out; we always over order and still manage to finish it all. On our very first date we went to a restaurant called Roka. Spen arrived late and was definitely not sober, but to be fair to him he had won *The Jump* the night before so had been OUT out. At the dinner I'd never seen ordering quite like it, the endless single glasses of champagne instead of saving some cash by ordering the bottle – it nearly sent me over the edge. It was a lovely date but at the end he realised he'd forgotten his wallet … I'm still sickened by the champagne bill. I really don't understand how restaurants get away with charging so much for it when you can get a bottle for a quarter of the price in a supermarket.

D'you know, I think I'm gonna start sneaking booze everywhere again.

Forgetting his wallet was not a red flag, though. From the very day I met him he has been so generous, but when he told me he had always paid for his partners it spurred me onto insist on going Dutch. How I wish I hadn't! Now I'll pay for half of everything for the rest of my life! I'm joking, I've always been very proud of standing on my own two feet and paying my way. When I had very little money I would stay out of big dinners or stay out of rounds if I couldn't afford them. A pal of mine, my God is she extravagant. (She still is but thankfully she doesn't live in this country any more so I don't have to remortgage my home to spend time with her.) When she would organise her birthday dinner, it would send shivers up all our spines. Dinner would always end up costing over 100 quid and for me at the time that was almost two nights out, so I would dread an invite from her. Some people just love to spend regardless of the cost and worry about the consequences later, but I've never been like that. I've always been conscious of what I spend and I still am, but not in the same way. Now, I just don't like being ripped off.

Spen was always paying for everyone's drinks. He didn't have a huge amount of money at the time, but he couldn't help himself. When we first started dating I noticed that people would take advantage of that and be quite expectant of him. He had a friend who had no money and Spen would always foot the bill when they went out and think nothing of it. Then his friend announced he had just bought a house. The same guy who said he didn't have a pot to piss in? He was happy for Spen to pay for everything when they were together so he could save his money for things he wanted to spend it on. Spen's not only generous when it comes to monetary things though, he's always been really generous with his time. We were in Battersea Park the other day and he went up to the café we always go to and they gave him a free coffee because they said he was always so nice and chatty. He is like a bat out of hell though, going at a million miles an hour. Sometimes I'll be at a meeting with him and I watch people's faces; they are windswept from the encounter. Or maybe they're just blown away by his breath because he was so close to them! The space invader strikes again.

We moved in together that October, nothing too unusual about that. By December I was pregnant with Theodore. In January Spen proposed and I said yes. Again, nothing too unusual – I do like a wedding and a marriage proposal is something you say yes to! I don't actually think that by the way. If for whatever reason this marriage doesn't work out (touch wood), I don't think I would get married again. I simply couldn't be bothered with the amount of planning that goes into it. I'd probably just have a big party and get Mary Black to come play at my house instead. I'd call it a 'We are mad about each other party' and leave it at that. This is the same plan I have for our ten-year anniversary, by the way; one way or another, I'm getting Mary Black to come to my house and sing.

The Christmas he proposed Spen was obsessed with *The Lion King* and I couldn't understand why he kept trying to get me to watch it. I was pregnant at the time, really tired and would fall asleep but he persisted each night. We all have our favourite Disney movies but mine is *Beauty and the Beast*; I would have happily watched that every night but no, more Lion King. Then he booked tickets to the stage show, such was his obsession. At this stage of the pregnancy I had severe morning sickness but I did manage to get through to the interval, at which point I said to Spen that we should leave because I was worried I would get sick in the middle of a show. Nope, leaving wasn't an option: Spen had booked us an access all areas tour after the show.

YIPPEEEEEE.

Spenno proposed to me on the stage at the Lyceum Theatre in front of four knackered lions from *The Lion King*, his favourite childhood film. I've been proposed to twice and this was still the better one.

Chapter Fourteen

Holliers

Williams Wilson Matthews … I certainly can't keep up so I don't expect you to either. Three names for one person – let me explain. I was born Vogue Williams and although I do go by that name it is no longer my legal surname. My legal surname is Wilson (although Spencer insists it's Matthews because I married him.) When I was around seventeen Neil made it clear he wanted me to change my name to Wilson as he was always booking flights, hotels, tickets, etc. and because he and my mom didn't like seeing my dad's surname on my passport. It was a constant reminder of how much they disliked him. Knowing it would mean a lot to them I went ahead and changed it, although I continued to use the name Williams because that's who I am. Cut to many years later and my true level of laziness shines through. While I should change my name back legally from Wilson to Williams (or to

Matthews, so there are fewer questions at the airport when I'm with the kids), I still haven't because changing my bills, bank accounts, passport and even that mini card passport is more admin than I'm willing to take on.

When Spen and I first got together I would see comments saying he had dragged me out of a trailer park. We don't really have the same class divide in Ireland so I found that whole conversation mystifying. Also, Spencer is posher than everyone, even his own family. Although he comes from a wealthy background his dad is self-made and very salt of the earth – no airs and graces, much like his mom, Jane, the Queen of Everything.

The first time I brought Spencer back to the homeland people were fascinated by his accent and I was too because in the nicest way possible it sounds completely ridiculous. He's the poshest person I've ever met in real life, my very own Lord Farquaad (from *Shrek*). It was like I had brought an alien to the Peninsula, but my family were quite taken with him all the same because he is great craic and very different to anyone else you might meet.

In the early days of meeting Spencer he constantly told me that I was going to be besties with his mother Jane. I'd never had a strong friendship with any of my ex's parents; not to say I disliked them (I wasn't mad about some of them), but I never built a friendship with any of them. I can only imagine how many people Spen had thrown at his mom before I was given my turn, but I loved her straight away. Jane is such a kind person and so welcoming; we became friends very quickly and I feel so lucky that I get to have a mother-in-law like her. Our families get on very well, my Aunty Jeana and my cousin spend Christmas with us each year up in Scotland at his parents' place, and I am happy to say there are no arguments over the TV or otherwise, although we Irish bring the noise for sure.

When Spen and I got married it couldn't have been more different from my first wedding. We decided to go down the registry office route and invited twenty-two of our closest friends and family to Spen's parents' place in Scotland – three days celebrating in the gorgeous Scottish sunshine. I was pregnant with Theodore at the time and we thought we'd have a big bash after he was born. Paul Costelloe made me a gorgeous simple gown for the day but the poor man had a serious job on his hands with my ever-changing body. For comfort I chucked on some gold sandals I had for years and did my own make-up, thinking I'll get Asho to do it when we have our real wedding. The weather was amazing, everyone was so relaxed and Glen Affric is one of the most beautiful places in the world, particularly when the sun is shining. Our cake was made by someone local, totally delicious, but had almost fallen over by the time we got to it because the temperature was so high – delighted for us! I would love to live that weekend again if I could. It was so good we decided that we didn't need to have another wedding, we had already had our perfect day and so decided to put our energies into setting up our home and enjoying Theodore. We didn't do a honeymoon, which I regret, but that's a difficult thing to do with a newborn!

Spen and I didn't have much time together as a couple before having kids and I would say they change the dynamic of your relationship. At times it's very difficult because having young kids is so full-on and often the last person you think of can be your partner. We try our best to be careful of that. Truly, this is my first relationship where my partner really feels like my friend. We talk about things we love, we laugh a lot together and in general we find so much enjoyment from just being together, even when we're doing nothing. Actually, especially when we're doing nothing.

We had gone to Thailand together before I fell pregnant with Theodore and it was the only two-week break we took in our relationship before having children, which is mad to think about. (Thailand still holds my record for the worst hangover I have ever had: SangSom rum in a bucket with concentrated Red Bull and a can of coke is not a drink I will ever have again. Please God stay away from the buckets in Thailand. I wish I'd gone to Mushy Mountain instead.)

One very memorable trip we enjoyed after we were married was to Amsterdam. If you haven't been to

Amsterdam, it's a beautiful city with amazing museums and is pretty progressive in terms of its laws around not only drugs but sex work too. When we were there, I was fascinated by the red-light district and the cafés. Coming from Ireland I had never seen anything like it. You can go one of two ways in Amsterdam; you can visit cafés and smoke weed for the day, or you can be a tourist in one of the best cities to be one in. On our first day there, Spen and I decided to 'take in the sights' and possibly enjoyed Amsterdam a little too early, which meant that the rest of the day went by in a blur. But we did make the most of that trip; we visited Anne Frank's House and The Van Gogh museum which is brilliant. Also the vintage shopping is whopper in Amsterdam and a bike tour is good craic too.

Spen and I invited two friends to join us and when they arrived it turned out one of the friends was on an entirely different holiday to us, but it made the trip a lot more interesting, to say the least. He is what you might call very sexually free and adventurous. Well, at least that's what he tells us, but I always think if you shout the loudest you must be covering up for something and that, in fact, he's probably very lazy in bed.

At that time he was in his 'trying to save people' phase, but when you try and save people who are quite happy it makes no sense to them or the pals watching behind your back. It all started innocently enough; we wandered through the red-light district and he decided he wanted to go in and chat with one of the girls. Chat he did: for almost two hours he was on the missing list, and when he finally returned, he told us how he had given his new friend 1,500 euro to change her life. It was sweet to be fair, but he couldn't get his head around the fact that she wanted to keep doing what she was doing. Another night he decided after a few drinks that we should go to a house party but I didn't really want to go because there were so many more fun places to go than someone's house.

After much begging we finally agreed to go for an hour. When we showed up to this random (but very gorgeous from the outside) house, we walked in and were brought down to a bar, which was brilliant. I couldn't believe someone had this in their house because it was so cool, but then things got weird very fast. Very shortly after our arrival I realised where we were; he had taken me and Spen (a married couple) and one of his friends to a brothel! It was nothing like I had imagined a brothel to be, but then when I began to properly look around and notice how people were behaving it all made sense. Our pal was shocked when we said we were leaving and it is still up there as one of the weirdest nights of my life. Two hours later he arrived home with one of the girls from the brothel and we had to then listen to him trying to save her from her life that she seemed to be quite happy with!

I haven't been back to Amsterdam since and I would never say never but it's not very high up on my list of places to visit any more. These days I'm more of a Seville or Lisbon girl.

Chapter Fifteen

The Three Little Pigs

When I became a thirty-year-old divorced woman, I had slightly given up my dreams of becoming a parent, which I now know is stupid. When I did find myself single at thirty I thought it was reasonable enough to believe I would never have children; sitting here at the age of thirty-nine considering my fourth child shows how stupid that was. Kids have changed my life so much and I feel so lucky to have them, but they're not for everyone and I can totally understand that; they upend your entire life and you quickly become the least important person and weirdly that doesn't matter – you don't want to put yourself above them. Until I had my own, I never knew the work that went into kids. That's when I really appreciated my own mother, who has four of us.

The mothering role is something I took on with people around me long before I had kids because I really like nothing more than looking after people wherever I can. Some people are maternal and I was always one of them; I had dolls that I treated as my human babies and that's all I really played with. No Barbies, it was a Baby Born or nothing. My dolls had everything a doll needed and I even started branching out into homeware, asking for ironing boards from Santa. Now I hate ironing, I'd rather clean the toilet than iron, but I loved it when I was young. Then I had baby Alzo, who I would borrow off my mom, which helped me really prepare for my future role as a mother.

When I first got pregnant I thought: This is fantastic, I finally have the boobs I've always wanted and a baby on the way.' After eight weeks of bliss it all went downhill pretty quickly and I was very sick until week thirty-two of my pregnancy. Feeling horrific, I would cry all the time and it's weird because you know you should be so happy but when you feel that sick it's hard to feel anything else. With Gigi and Otto I was sick up until the day I had them so I always say I feel amazing after giving birth. It's not because I'm some earth mother, it's because for the first time in months I can remember what it's like to feel normal and I love it.

When I was in the early stages of pregnancy I was diagnosed with hyperemesis gravidarum, which is severe nausea and vomiting, although I skipped the vomiting which I guess was good. All day and all night I would feel so sick. It helped to sleep sitting up but my God it's a very difficult thing to go through. It felt like the only thing I ever said during that time was 'I feel sick'; I must have driven everyone mad with my whinging. When all you can think about is how sick you feel, it's all you can talk about too! Without the tablets I was prescribed I would have been completely bedbound. At first I didn't want to take those bad boys because I heard they could affect the baby (that used to happen years ago), but thankfully that was in the past and medical science has come a long way since then.

Usually, once I hit the twelve-week mark, I'd start to feel slightly better for parts of the day and start eating everything around me. I love hearing about other people's cravings when they're pregnant so I'll throw mine at you. I totally understand if it's a snorefest, but at the very least it might give you ideas for dinner. Theodore had quite a few cravings, one being bruschetta, which was fanbloodytastic for my heartburn (not!). The whole pregnancy I tried so hard to resist but the draw of tomatoes on bread became too much and another prescription for severe heartburn would inevitably ensue. Another craving had to be done in secret; I wasn't one of those people who start eating rocks or sofas, it was actually worse than that. I became addicted to sushi. You are not supposed to eat sushi at all but to be honest I think some of these rules are a load of crap. I highly doubt women in Japan stop

189

eating sushi so what's the problem? I would however draw the line at oysters, only because I was so ill once after a dodgy one and you don't need more reasons to feel ill during pregnancy.

Soft cheese is another banned substance I craved. It's difficult enough for pregnant women, we have to give up everything, but I'm sorry but I am not giving up cheese. Again I'm going by the rule that if French women are okay I would be fine too. When I was pregnant with Gigi I couldn't get enough of Dip Dabs (a cheap red lollipop in a bag of sherbet). There wasn't enough sherbet in the world to satisfy that craving, so I bought them in boxes of fifty. It got pretty bad and as soon as Gigi was born I never wanted to see a Dip Dab again. The only problem was that everyone started giving me Dip Dabs all the time to be nice, even though I couldn't bear the sight of them. With Otto it was oranges. I did consider leaving it at oranges, but if I'm totally honest there were a good few boxes of Flumps. I don't think I overdid it on the Flumps because if I spot them in a shop I'll still pick them up. (The best shops in Ireland sell Flumps, fizzy Chewits and Golf Balls chewing gum.)

As someone who is always tired even when I'm working off eight hours of sleep, the levels of tiredness when I was pregnant were awful. I thought I would never be able to get through a full day but then when I hit my second trimester I didn't even feel pregnant any more. Pregnancy has the weirdest symptoms and I was so happy I had a friend who had gone through it before me so she could warn me about them. The weirdest pregnancy thing of all for me was the fat vagina. I am talking size up a couple of sizes in your knickers by trimester three because the lips will need some extra room. It terrified me and I insisted my doctor take a look at my Fionnuala every time I went in for a check-up. She would always try and explain that it was normal but I wouldn't believe that mine could possibly be a normal size and I needed the reassurance that it would go back down. Strangely enough, when there isn't a baby weighing down on your pelvis it does go back to normal size.

Childbirth isn't easy on anybody but I did enjoy it – wait, maybe that's the wrong way of putting it – I would take childbirth over being pregnant any day, and there are parts of it I actively enjoyed. A particular highlight for me was the gas and air and it makes me feel sad that one day I won't have any more babies and therefore I won't have any more gas and air. The first time I had it was when I fell off a horse and needed stitches; they gave it to me when they cleaned out my wound and WOW what a buzz. I even tried to buy some on Amazon as they were working on me because I thought this is the greatest thing anyone ever invented. What I didn't realise was that it can be quite dangerous if used improperly and is not something that can be freely bought online. Just so you know.

During childbirth they give you almost free rein of the machine though, and it has to be said it's very useful for pain relief and fun too; at times I felt like I was at a festival and would have to ask the doctor to come back and repeat what she'd just said because it's very difficult to talk to someone rationally when you've just taken a blast. I was all for the epidural as well. Initially, of course, I had thoughts of going through labour without it but eventually took the view that if someone were to chop my arm off and offer to do it with or without pain relief I would choose pain relief. I apply the same logic to childbirth.

The day of giving birth is all about the mother, it's fantastic and I relish that kind of attention. Sometimes if I'm sick I wish I could be in hospital with people looking after me and giving me gas and air. All three of my babies have been induced, which means that I'm an impatient bitch and I wanted to meet them early, although Theodore was overdue and my vagina couldn't wait a moment longer.

Gigi wasn't moving as much so we got worried, but I wouldn't say she moves much even now. Poor baby Otto was ten days early because his father decided to go to Everest base camp for five weeks and you can only do that in May, so he had to come early to meet his dad! It's funny because you can sort of choose your child's date of birth when you get induced. If I hadn't googled dates in

April Otto could have shared a birthday with Hitler. The horror! We sidestepped that quite quickly.

The day you get to bring your baby home is the absolute best. We went home with T after one day, we were just so excited to bring him back. He had this massive cone head because his labour was quite difficult. I had been rushed to the emergency room to have a C-section but at the last minute I was able to have him vaginally (helped out with a suction device, hence the cone head). One little tip. Don't let your husband send your family the first set of pictures. Spencer sent Theodore in his full cone head glory to my mom at 4 a.m. and she couldn't go back to sleep because she thought something had happened to him.

One of the most annoying things about being a new mother was how when anyone came over they would tell me to take a nap. I must have looked like I was around ninety and in dire need of sleep because it was relentless, and when you get home all you want to do is hold your baby. Oh and eat pastries and cakes. Usually, I could go quite a long time without a cinnamon bun, but when I was breastfeeding I wanted them all the time.

Kids are hilarious. My kids have me in stitches all the time with some of the stuff they come out with and their wobblers can be outrageous. I once took T to the park during his terrible twos and the lovely man mowing the lawn offered him a go on the tractor. 'This will be nice,' I thought and it was – until the time came to take T off the tractor! My pal was with me and she had no kids so when she witnessed the meltdown the shock in her face was very funny to me. I was used to it; she was most definitely not. Another time Hadley my hairdresser was over (he doesn't have kids either) when Kid A scratched a scab off the back of Kid B, throwing Kid B into utter meltdown, convinced this would be the end of them. That took a lot of calming down and then once the kids were sorted I had to calm Hadley down – he'd never seen anything quite like it.

Like I've said, some of my parenting style comes from my own parents, although I am yet to be as lethal on the chores as Sandra and Neil were. Otherwise I do my own thing, whatever comes naturally. All I want is for my children to be happy, well-mannered, kind kids. I accept that they will at times fail at all these things during their lifetimes, but don't we all? We did give our kids iPads so they could have some TV at night and the amount of time they watched it always ended up being extended because, let's be honest, iPads make life easier. Recently, however, we took the iPads off them and it's the one thing that has made such a huge difference to their behaviour. They still get to watch TV, but they aren't as interested so they play a lot more now. I'm not giving parenting advice because I don't think anyone should, but if your kids have a lot of screen time try reducing it if you can; it's been amazing for us.

Theodore is my eldest son and he is incredibly smart and really kind and although he can throw a complete wobbler at home, it's never witnessed out in the wild (bar tractorgate). He's addicted to knowing everything about animals and I have learned so much from our nightly googling; every night he gets to choose one animal to hear facts about before bed. He also knows the names of every dinosaur, most of which I never even knew existed. He's kind and caring towards his siblings and loves trying to frighten me because I once told him a story of how I used to hide under my mom's bed when she was getting ready for a night out – I would choose my moment and then grab her leg, scaring the absolute shite out of her. Theodore is always lurking ready to grab a leg and it's my own doing.

Gigi is her own girl. She loves anything pink and would happily play with adults all day, forgoing making any new friends of her own. On holiday she just hangs out with Aunty Naomi and doesn't bother making any friends, despite a lot of offers. She adores dressing up and is very funny but doesn't like if you laugh at her, which makes you laugh even more. She sizes everyone up and can take some time to adjust to new people, but everyone wants to be pals with Gigi.

Otto, my little man, does whatever he wants. He is in charge of our household currently and spends his time singing nursery rhymes. It's fascinating to hear him sing with all the words because he's only two. Kids have no chill, absolutely none. They can't just sit in and watch movies, they have to be out or occupied 90 per cent of the time. As a parent I really thought there would be a lot more Disney in my life but most of my time is spent in a park with them.

The kids have better social lives than us now, at least two parties a week and three different activities on a weekend. Kids' parties are on a different level in London, forget the Party Rings and Mikado biscuits. We are talking wood-fired pizza and crudités with hummus vibes. I know people that have spent fortunes on their kids' parties, but I like to set myself a goal of having a great party while spending as little as possible. I wouldn't even spend what some people spend on a first birthday party on my fortieth! Saying that, we did get bitten by the first birthday party bug with Theodore – only because we didn't know any better. We had a petting zoo that T had zero interest in but all the adults I invited loved it. Theodore's name may have been on the invite, but it definitely felt like a Spencer and Vogue party.

One thing I am very good at is kids' presents because I just buy all the toys I would have wanted as a child. People are always horrified when they spot the presents I leave out for the kids at Christmas or birthdays in my stories because I never wrap them. I just can't bring myself to wrap a load of gifts. It was never done for me and that's a family tradition I'm willing to stick to. As much as possible I try to avoid kids' parties but that can't always be achieved. Our nanny who works with us usually takes whoever is going to the party and I will take the other kids to the park.

Our schedule with the kids is intense and I know I overdo it but we have walked every inch of Battersea Park and as great as it is, we can't spend all our waking moments in there. It can be pretty hard making sure all the kids get to everything they have on, but where I can manage it they do things together. This weekend we had three kids' parties, a trip to softplay, tennis and swimming and next week their gymnastics starts up, so our weekends mainly consist of kid stuff.

They're very active and T in particular loves running so he does run club and athletics midweek. It can be quite demoralising to be outrun by a six-year-old, but it's a regular occurrence for me. Sometimes I think: 'Let's not do athletics or pottery or football, let's take a day off,' but they really like it and it's good for them to try things. I'm hoping in time they'll all choose a couple of things a week to concentrate on and that will be that. It's a very different childhood to mine; I don't think we did anything at their age, it just wasn't the way things were. We got sent out to play at weekends, would come back for lunch and head back out again until dinner. Still, I always felt like I had an incredibly busy schedule thanks to Amber. Of course we got taken to the carnival or the cinema but it certainly wasn't a weekly thing.

We have always had a nanny for our kids. I didn't want to send them to nursery as babies because I work from home a lot and whenever I have time off I want to be able to spend it with the kids. If I had a 9–5 job in an office that would make sense, but for our lifestyle having a nanny works better. There are always so many opinions floating around about nannies and I find it strange because it's like you're expected to either work or look after your kids and doing both at the same time just isn't an option.

I grew up with au pairs my whole life as my mom had two jobs, one of which was as an air hostess, so she needed that help. I don't know if it was frowned on back then, but if it was, I don't think my mom would have taken much notice. Our nannies (they alternate) feel like an extension of our family and I think we will always keep in contact, even when they don't work with us any more. The kids love them and we love them – you can't ask for much more than that.

A friend told me lately that a mutual friend of ours was pretty disgusted about the fact that I had a nanny and didn't think I was being a good mother because of it. At the same time her child was in daycare from 8 a.m. until she finished work. I'm aware that's a reality for a lot of people who don't work from home but the hypocrisy did make me laugh. I know I'm a great mother. I'll always be grateful that I can do things that I couldn't if I didn't have help.

Most mornings I wake up just before 7 a.m. and the first thing I'll do is snuggle Gigi, who has snuck into our bed even though she promised she wouldn't just mere hours ago. Otto will always be screaming Mama, waiting for me to come in and get him, then T gets up and joins us in the kitchen, where we catch up on each other's dreams. Usually by the time I've fed the dogs and given Winston his medication our nanny has arrived and I go downstairs for a 30-minute workout. (Sometimes I take T to run club super early so I don't train before that.) Back upstairs I help the kids get ready and aim to be out the door with three kids and two dogs by 8 a.m. I love walking the kids to school and nursery, and collecting them too, when I can. It sets up our days perfectly and the goal is always to be able to do at least one of them on any given day.

Once I've dropped off T and Gigi I take Otty home and try to get myself ready really quickly for whatever work I have on that day. If I've no morning jobs I'll take Otty to nursery. Recently, I've started getting him to scoot or cycle to nursery, which makes it a long old trek, after which I feel like I've a broken back. That's my dream morning, but it's not the same every day as sometimes I'm away with work and don't get to do drop off (although my management does try to give me most mornings off to do drop off.) The rest of the day is work. I'll cycle into Global, where I record most of my podcasts, work from home or head off to any other jobs I've on at the time. I usually finish around 5 p.m. in time to help with dinner, bath and homework time. There's a lot to fit in with work and the kids so I do find myself working again once I get them down but I'll finish up by 8 p.m., as I tend to start shutting down around then.

While I do feel guilty when I'm not with my children, honestly, spending every waking moment with children would send any sane person over the edge. When I'm not with them I miss them so deeply my heart physically hurts, but sometimes on a Saturday after swimming and two kids' parties I think a little me time wouldn't go amiss. Sometimes if it's been a very full-on week, I will watch our nanny leave and think how lovely and quiet her house must be and dream about jumping into her bag and sneaking into the silent retreat she calls home!

There are always so many stories flying around that you can't do it all and I really hate that. Why can't you? Why can't you have kids and still keep the career you love? I love working but I do get guilt when I have to go away. But guess what? I LOVE when I go away for work too. I understand that life is hectic and at times I feel like I can't do it all, but then I give myself a good talking to and we are back on track.

One rule I have is that unless absolutely necessary I will never spend more than three nights away from the kids; it's too much for me and for them. When I went to Australia on tour with *My Therapist Ghosted* Me, I was away for ten days and while I loved it I couldn't have lasted one more day. It's a constant juggle and a struggle but whatever way you do it you can make it work, although something will always suffer. For me it's the amount of time I get to spend with friends. Fortunately, I work with a lot of friends and I have lots of friends who have kids, so those worlds often collide too. I also have friends who would rather not hang out with my kids and I think that's fair enough.

When I became a mother, I think I lost a part of my old self. I don't mean that in a bad way, it's just the truth. The carelessness I used to have and the times I could feel like I had no responsibilities is gone. When I was away in Australia it felt really weird to walk around and do whatever I wanted for ten whole days! I love being a mother but I want to try and be myself too as much as I can.

Our kids are quite well-behaved but we do have time-outs for when they aren't. Otto finds this hilarious and although he is currently too young to be put in time-out he likes to go around and point fingers at everyone, telling them they will be put in time out. Spencer and I definitely have different parenting skills. I believe that a schedule and some rules are important, whereas Spencer would believe that anything that brings peace makes more sense. I don't mind deviating from the schedule sometimes – if we are on holiday or maybe over the weekend – but Spencer would deviate at all times.

Theodore has copped onto who is the easier parent. He will ask me for something and if I say no, I will hear him head off to the kitchen and ask Spen and get an immediate yes. I wouldn't say I'm a strict parent; I just think that very young kids like knowing what's coming up next and that works best with our children. They have TV and eat sweets but it's all in moderation. I'm not here to tell them they can't have sweets when I eat a mountain of them myself. As much as possible I try my best to put myself in their position when they are demanding things, and remember I was like that too.

We recently went to Theodore's parent-teacher meeting and there have been question marks around his attention span. This is of no surprise to either of us – I have the worst attention span of us all. Sometimes I will ask Spen a question and then walk off while he's answering it, like I'm bored of his answer so my brain tells me to leave. While I do have attention problems, I find them to be the problems of others – if you can keep me interested then I will listen and take things in, but if you decide to be boring there is a strong chance I will switch off.

Okay, so maybe I need to work on some areas, but none us is meant to be perfect. My poor stepdad looks after my finances and when he has to call me to go through stuff I sit there pinching myself trying not to drift off. Aside from a touch of ADHD and a dash of OCD, I think I'm a pretty well put-together person. I have never been tested for ADHD; the test is hours long and how anyone with attention problems is expected to sit through something like that is beyond me, but my therapist thinks it would be a good idea. A pal of mine takes Adderall for their ADHD, which sounds eerily similar to the effects of cocaine.

One of my toughest times as a mother was when Theodore was almost eighteen months and we decided to try for another baby. We knew we wanted one but were petrified at the thought of another child to look after. I think it's always scary because it is hard and you wonder how well you will cope. We had a very early miscarriage and it's not something I've ever talked about before because it was so early on and, if I'm honest, I didn't feel like I had the right to be whinging, especially as I've had friends who lost babies very late into their pregnancy. Still, it was a shock and very unexpected because you think you're super healthy and nothing could go wrong but it did. We were in our friends' house in France at the time, chatting in the kitchen and I felt a huge gush (sorry for the graphics). I ran to the toilet and I just knew straight away … there was a lot of cramping and bleeding for days afterwards.

When we got home to London I went to the clinic for confirmation and they did confirm it, but in the least sympathetic way. The doctor did the scan and just announced, 'Yes, that was a miscarriage, see ya later, bye.' I suppose they are used to it but a bit of a nicer bedside manner would have been really appreciated. My doctor in Ireland is the ideal candidate for this scenario: no bullshit, to the point, gets the job done but also has sympathy, even though she must be fed up with all the whingers that cross her path.

Even though we already had a happy, healthy baby it was a difficult time and I'm glad Spen and I were able to navigate that on our own. Fortunately for us, not long afterwards I was pregnant again. We had to wait until our ten-week scan to determine the sex of the baby. At the scan our doctor didn't want to guess, but we insisted and she said at that very early stage that it was a boy.

Obviously the health of our baby was the most important thing, but there was still a twinge of 'Oh, I wish it was a girl!' Cut to a few weeks later when we got the test results back and BOOM. Never have I been happier to know a doctor was in fact wrong! It was a girl after all, our Gigibear. We were so happy to have a girl after a boy, it was the icing on the cake and little Gigi is a total winner. Almost two years later Otto was up next for us and although we are still considering a fourth child, three can be a lot!

Spen and I go through our moments when thinking of having another one. Sunday just gone it was a definite no; yesterday I would have been well up for baby four.

I realise what I am about to write will sound insane to some people but I go and see a girl who is a clairvoyant and she was the one who told me I was pregnant with a girl long before I even knew I was pregnant with Gigi. At the time I remember thinking she was being quite insensitive considering what we had just gone through with the miscarriage, but she insisted she was right and she was. Recently, she told me we would have one more girl … but let's wait and see.

Chapter Sixteen

Bumps in the Road

Spencer once said to me that my mood can dictate the tone of our house. He said it one morning because I woke up tired and not my usual self. Everyone has the right to have their bad days but I'm a firm believer in not letting your bad day affect anyone else's. Putting a dampener on anyone else's day because you're in a stinker is a big no-no. After he told me that I really took it on board and even on days where I feel crap I'll plaster a smile to my face and try to moan in private. It's not like I'm totally masking my feelings, just putting them to one side for a more appropriate time. Nobody is on good form 100 per cent of the time, but I would be in a great mood most of the time and a bad mood rarely. Being a woman there are times in the month where you don't feel great – I only started tracking my period when I was in my late thirties and it really is like clockwork. I'm irritable about a week before it, I just want to be left alone and then I'm fine the week it arrives. Hormones are tricky because you can't really do anything about the way they make you feel, but at least you can discover the source of your feelings.

Although it comes and goes, anxiety is still such a big part of my life and sometimes I really can't stand it because I can't explain it and I don't know where it comes from. When Theodore was born it wasn't that my anxiety was heightened, it was more that my worrying increased because now there was someone – far more important than myself – who I had to protect at all costs. We were on holiday in St Barths (very relatable, I know, but any time I try to make it seem more relatable by pointing out that my husband grew up there, that seems to make it worse!). Anyway, it's a very hilly island and we would take T for walks up and down some extremely steep hills and there was a voice going through my mind, my own voice, telling me not to let go of the buggy. On and on and on it went until finally I reached the end of the hill where I high-fived myself for not letting go of the buggy. Weird.

Recently we went on a couples' holiday to the Amalfi coast, somewhere I've always wanted to go. But the day before we left, I had this awful guilty feeling that I shouldn't be going because the following week I had a work trip and that would mean too much time away from the kids. Once we arrived, we had a great day: a lovely massage, an early dinner with no booze – the perfect concoction for a great night's sleep – or so I thought. Just as I was about to fall asleep, I started to spiral for a bit but managed to control it enough to fall asleep. Then I woke up with a jolt when Spen made a noise and I thought something had happened – well, that was the end of the road for me and sleep! I was awake until 4 a.m. but not comfortably awake, so I did my usual routine: had a beta-blocker, read my book, took a Piriton, did breathing techniques; none of it worked. I cried on and off from the frustration, feeling embarrassed because Spen doesn't get anxiety and so I assumed he must have been thinking I was INSANE.

Wrapped up in a dressing gown that felt like a hug, I went onto the balcony and wrote down what was causing me this anxiety, then went back into the room to test out sleeping again with an eye mask, ear plugs and a pillow over my face (I feel safer when I'm enclosed). Eventually I fell asleep but woke up four hours later, presumably because the beta-blocker had worn off and my heart was thumping through my chest. I really wished I'd had a Xanax, but getting some from a doctor is almost impossible; you'd be better off calling a drug dealer. The next day my pulse was still up to ninety so I took a beta-blocker, tried to train the feeling out of my body and planned a pharmacy trip so I'd have some kind of sleeping tablet available to me if it happened again. Anything is better than nothing, even if it is just some herbal thing.

I hate my anxiety and I can imagine it can sometimes be difficult to be with someone who has it to the extent I do. Spen is patient for the most part, but when we are away trying to spend time as a couple I'm sure he finds it frustrating that I can't just relax and enjoy myself without worrying about the kids. We have made a promise to each other to spend time away together, at least one weekend a year. So far I've spent most of those weekends talking, thinking and getting anxious about the kids. Something to work on for sure.

One of the biggest problems Spen and I have encountered in our marriage have been because of booze, and he won't mind me saying that as he's been very honest with himself about it. It nearly ended our marriage on a couple of occasions but luckily for us we were able to navigate our way through it. The first time we had issues was when I was pregnant with Theodore. Spen was drinking heavily and maybe it was more noticeable to me because we now lived together and I wasn't drinking. The thing about people who drink is that it's not just the day that they drink that's annoying (if you don't feel like getting involved), but it's also their mood for days after. Most of the week he was either in bad form or drunk, and I didn't like it. I'm not interested in spending time with someone who's in bad form because they're hungover and have not slept well. (I can be like that myself but I really try not to be when I'm hungover, because it's my own fault.) One of the reasons I never like being hungover around my kids is because you definitely have less patience and it's not fair to be snappy around them. It got so bad with Spen at this time that I couldn't even trust him to take the dogs for a walk when I wasn't at home.

It was also very difficult watching him waste his time; I could see potential in Spen that he couldn't see in himself. Neither did I want my future to be with a husband who didn't do a lot, didn't achieve what he could and was drunk far too often. It's not attractive when someone does very little with themselves because they'd rather sit at home and drink. Knowing I couldn't have that in my life for ever, I explained to him that I wouldn't be hanging around if that was what he wanted to do. I wasn't giving Spen an ultimatum; it's impossible to try and get someone to change – I had learned that in the past. I simply explained to him that I couldn't continue if he wanted to carry on as he was.

He knew he wasn't achieving what he could and now he could see that he would lose me and our life together so he decided to quit drinking. Even though I could see what Spenno could achieve and how the booze was blocking him, it was something he had to figure out for himself. I feel so incredibly proud that he was able to do it. He went from drinking to being – well, in the nicest way possible – sanctimonious about NOT drinking, but I was all for it. That was how he had to do it and it

211

completely changed all of our lives. I feel really fortunate that he was able and willing to do that for us, that we were important enough to him to want to change. One of Spen's regrets is his speech at our wedding; he wishes he was sober at the time because his speech wasn't what he had hoped it would be. In a way I wish he had been sober then too, or at least the way he is now (where he can have the odd drink and not go wild) because he's a much better version of himself, but I'm not walking down the aisle again. It's greedy and I can't expect anyone to want to come to yet another wedding!

Spen's true nature is so focused, career-driven and ambitious and it was all just hidden in a hazy hangover. I find him fascinating in that sense; his ability to achieve whatever he sets his mind to is wild. He started a non-alcoholic booze brand CleanCo and he would never have done that had he not given up drinking. Recently he ran thirty marathons in thirty days in the Jordanian desert, all for charity. Imagine how hideous it would be to run one marathon, let alone one every single day for thirty days? No thank you! Whenever I see people having issues in life, if they come to me for any kind of advice (I honestly don't like giving advice unless it's asked for because that is very annoying), I will usually start by telling them to take some time off drinking and to exercise more; getting some clarity, in my opinion, is a great start to addressing areas of your life that aren't working that well for you. I do this when I have really bad anxiety and it's the only way I can help myself. I don't think I could ever give up booze completely but at the same time I really want to because I just hate how it makes me feel the next day. But then I remember it's a lot of fun and I like to let loose every so often – you do need something. Maybe I'll take up drugs – that's a good idea, just a little occasional weed or something. Sandra, if you're reading this, that was a joke: drugs are bad, kids.

If I wasn't so cynical I would say, yes, this marriage is going to be for ever but you just never know what's going to happen. I have an awful habit of deciding that the whole thing is over after an argument; it's a protective tactic. Assume the worst and then it won't be so bad. Or I could die tomorrow and he could pull a Clint Eastwood and meet someone mere days after the funeral, or even at the funeral – I can only imagine the amount of women keen to make him feel better! I know it sounds awful, but when you've been in a lot of long-term relationships and they all end, it's more realistic to think they will all go the same way. I do believe, though, that I have met someone I want to spend the rest of my life with and I feel very fortunate. Both our parents have been together a long time and that's what I hope for us, although I do wonder how they don't get fed up with each other. Maybe after that long people become an extension of you and you of them.

Of course, if he annoys me then he's getting the boot pronto. It's hard to get on my bad side, but even I wouldn't want to find myself there. I can confirm it's not a nice place to be. I am so stubborn that I would cut my nose off to spite my face and I don't back down very easily. On the flip side, however, I do very little to be annoying. (This is my opinion – I like to have my own back, but if I had to be honest, then fine, sometimes I'm annoying.)

Spencer has told me that he thinks one day I will turn around and decide I want an open relationship; he believes that I will want to spread my wings and go on a wild sexual adventure. I thought long and hard about that and even approached the idea with my therapist, but I just don't think it's in the stars for me; I'm more of a long-term team player. I'll either stay happily married or start up my own sex cult where you can only join if you are really funny or an 8/10, and once you're in you can never leave. It would also be important that you're an exceptionally tidy and organised person and we would all have a ball (or ten). Sorry, I couldn't help myself.

Chapter Seventeen

The Biz

I really see everything as an experience and have enjoyed most of my journey in the biz to date. Jobs aren't that plentiful at the start of anyone's freelance career but even more so in the industry I'm in. So when I was offered jobs I took them, was professional and I got it done. If it involved trawling a weird beach in London picking up rubbish with Peppa Pig then so be it! Actually, that one was recent enough but it had a charity element and my kids loved Peppa so it was a no-brainer until I saw the pictures … now, they were a sight to behold. If you google it you'd be right in thinking 'What the fuck is she wearing?' The worst thing about the internet is that nothing ever dies, it lives on for ever and ever. Sometimes if papers are writing something about me, they will dredge up the most rotten picture they can find and print it. Sneaky.

In Ireland I did a show about sex that took me to a sex party at an industrial estate in County Offaly – doesn't sound very sexy does it, although they did have a swing and the place reeked of Dettol so you knew it was clean. People showed up with their partners ready to swap them; a lot of the women were hot but the men not so much, they were clearly getting the better deal. There were even some wankers around the place. I call them that because they just watch and wank! I didn't see any of the activities going on but there was certainly a vibe happening before I left. For another part of that show I found myself in a sex dungeon in London that people rent out and I have never seen so many sex toys that are all reused by other people. I'm sorry but I draw the line at using a stranger's butt plug. Whatever you're into, but at least bring your own equipment!

There were plenty more embarrassing moments to come in my career, but it's important to lean in and enjoy what you're doing. When I was asked to horserace in the charity Goodwood race, I jumped at the chance, forgetting I had totally forgotten even the basics of horse riding. (I did some lessons as a teenager but quit early.) As an Irish person it's too confusing to me to simply say 'ride' a horse as 'ride' has a double meaning in Ireland, and that's NOT what I'm doing to horses.

Training was at a stable in Epsom near my house but I had seriously miscalculated the amount of time I would have to give towards this job. Four days a week I had to leave my house at 5 a.m., not returning home until 1 p.m. My first day I went up to what they call a gallop, where the horses can go at any speed you ask them to in as straight a line as you can achieve to prepare them and you for racing. I just clung on for dear life.

Thankfully I improved and really enjoyed myself until it came to choosing my horse for the real race. We went up to a huge stable in York where they had hundreds of horses. The horse who was kindly letting me race on him was certainly not pleased to see me at all. He was kicking his stable door, trying to bite me and if he could have trampled on me I'm quite sure he would have – if I didn't love horses so much I would call him a prick because that is what he was. Off to the gallop we went and all was going swimmingly until the horse behind me reared up and frightened my horse, causing him to bolt. When that happens you're fucked – sit and suffer is the saying. Every attempt to stop him was futile. I was clinging on tightly to the reins trying to get him to stop but to him that meant 'go faster'. (Unfortunately, I hadn't learned that yet.) Off we went, faster and faster, until he took a sharp left turn and I landed flat on my back. Never have I been so winded in my life; I honestly thought I was going to die because I couldn't get the air back into my lungs. Because I was concentrating so much on breathing I didn't even notice my arm. When I could finally breathe again next up was the excruciating pain in my arm. Blood everywhere.

It wasn't broken, but I needed twelve stitches and – silver lining – I got my first blast of gas and air. I left York defeated but returned two weeks later to try out my new 'kinder horse'. Gentle or kind he was not! He was acting very pissy in the stable, but the owner insisted he was lovely and besides we were off to a grass racecourse where if the horse ran away with me he would eventually run out of steam. No bother. Unsurprisingly, the horse knew I was a crap rider so he seized his moment. I didn't feel as worried this time because we were on grass, but how wrong I was. I ended up on my back in a bush with the worst whiplash. The horse was also in the bush and the trainer said that in his forty-year career he had never seen that happen, which I took as a compliment. In the end I came sixth in the race and now I'm a lot more careful about what I choose to do for work.

Mainstream TV shows in the UK are few and far between so landing one is always a big deal, but I do look back at some I said yes to and silently wish I hadn't. Unless you know everything about everything *Mastermind* is a fool's game and fool I was, skipping on set in my gorgeous patterned dress, blissfully unaware of how stupid I would seem. You choose your favourite topic to answer questions on; my original choice was rap music and it's important you know that because it will soften the blow when you find out what my topic ultimately was. Unfortunately for me they had previously had a special episode on rap music so I had to choose something else.

As a naturally competitive person I chose something I know absolutely everything about, Kim Kardashian. Did I nail the Kim K questions? Yes, I certainly did. 'I'm amazing,' I thought, as I galloped through them getting every question right. 'What a clever cookie, I can hold my head up high when I leave these studios.' So full of positivity was I, I had a literal spring in my step. At least I did until they landed me with the general knowledge questions. Before you judge, I would like to show a few of those questions here and get your thoughts.

Which actor best known for his film portrayal of a boy wizard played Rosencrantz in a 2017 London production of *Rosencrantz and Guildenstern Are Dead*? I even had to google that now, some of us don't watch Harry Potter! Master James of St George designed many buildings for Edward I that are still standing in North Wales. What are those buildings? Now this is a very sneaky question, if they had asked me about Ireland I may have known.

What a load of crap! It didn't deter people from assuming I was the thickest plank of wood to ever leave Ireland. The country certainly wouldn't want me back after that display – I was England's problem now! Slightly embarrassing moment but one I will live down. The cheeky bastards asked me back on the show not long ago. It was a polite no. By the way, if you got those questions right I think you'd be better off reading something by Stephen Fry than Vogue Williams!

The big Saturday night shows are always a laugh and one such show is *Family Fortunes*. I've done it twice and it's a great one to be offered. The first one I did was with my old family (first husband) and so I thought it was only right to do one with my new family. Now I'm just waiting for them to bring back *Mr and Mrs* – I definitely have one more episode of that in me. *Family Fortunes* is a cheese-fest: big smiles, big waves, etc. and when I watch it back it certainly looks a little cheesy and chaotic, but it's so much fun and I really don't feel the need to try and look cool all the time. A cool life must be exhausting, and one I don't want any part of.

My gang are cool AF and we don't need to be seen in the right places or be with the right people because when you're happy where you are it doesn't matter. I know people that would literally climb mountains to be seen with certain people. I probably had a touch of that in my younger years, but I look at people who are desperately trying to look cool now and feel a bit sorry for them. They probably feel sorry for me too, so there's a lot of sympathy going around.

I'm always dipping my toe in and out of reality TV but I think for the most part I am done now. Spen and I got offered a show recently, but I just want to concentrate on hosting so I'll wait for the right gig to come along. The big dream for me is still the shiny floor show or a big Saturday night chat show. While writing this book I actually secured a job hosting a show called *Renovation Rescue*. I'm really excited to begin work on it because I'll finally be doing something useful with my construction degrees!

Podcasting was an obvious choice, although it came quite late in the day for me, which is a shame because I love talking so I wish I'd gotten into it sooner. My first pod, *Spencer and Vogue*, I co-hosted with my husband. Such an inventive name, right? It was lovely to be able to work together; we don't get to spend that much time together because we're both so busy so it was a lot of fun. Of course, sometimes things would get a little spicy, which is bound to happen when you're working with your husband and Spencer has thrown quite a few epic wobblers down the years. He was especially not happy when I slagged the onion painting he did when he was sixteen years old. Every so often he would threaten to quit, but these are the usual conflicts and dramas of a married couple. (For the record, though, I WAS ALWAYS RIGHT.)

In 2024, he decided to take a step back from the pod to concentrate on his solo projects. Towards the end he did very little work for it anyway and it didn't feel much like a team effort so I felt it was time to give him the boot. Joking … sort of! What I like about podding is talking about light-hearted, easy and fun topics, whereas Spenny wanted to do more serious content. Towards the end the energy in the studio wasn't the same and neither were the laughs. We had planned his exit months in advance but as soon as the news came out everyone decided we were getting a divorce. No matter what we said we could not get journalists to believe that we weren't so it went on for quite some time, which was interesting in one sense; I suppose we did have a divorce but it was only a work divorce on the pod. We will, of course, work together on something again.

When Spencer left I decided to continue the pod with my sister Amber: she's so much fun and we have that sibling vibe; it feels like a great step. When I pod I like to have fun with my co-hosts and guests, laughing and slagging each other (very important) and that's the way I want to keep it. Amber took to it like a duck to water: well, a little flap around at the start but after that she was all good. (I had to pretend I needed her to step in for a bonus episode that Spen couldn't do so we could test her out.) I love being with Amber so it's been great to work with her and long may it last. If she messes up I can always kick her in the gee again!

A great friend of mine, Joanne McNally, moved to London and we became close. We were having a lot of fun together so one day I roped her into doing an Insta live with me. We filmed her doing my tan (her tanning skills have since improved) and that video did very well, so we began to think of ways we could work together. The obvious one was a pod. The first time we went into the studio together we really didn't know how we would gel. With some people it has been really difficult, mainly because they won't shut up so you're listening to a monologue from them and it's boring for any listener. Luckily, Joanne and I listened to each other and enjoyed each other's conversation and so the pod worked. It was a wise decision to have an edit in place too, because we do tend to go off on some tangents and there have been quite a few cancellable (unaired) moments.

We never thought *My Therapist Ghosted Me* would go as well as it has, but I will be forever grateful for what it did for my career. I didn't realise it before, but people thought I was quite straight-laced and possibly a little boring from what they had seen of me online. That's the great thing about podcasts, because they are so personal you have more of a stake in them and so tend to give a lot more of yourself. I've always been exactly how I am in real life on my podcasts. After a year of releasing episodes we decided to tour *MTGM* Live. Doing live stage shows is something I never thought I would do ever again because, years earlier, I was in a play in the biggest theatre in Dublin and I'm so happy that went under the radar because it was not a career highlight. First of all, I had to sing even though

I can't sing and second of all my family kept coming to the show so I was scarlet. I like acting but I'd much rather act in anonymity than in front of my family, who still slag me off for it. On the opening night I had to pretend to have an orgasm based on the famous scene from the movie *When Harry Met Sally*. My parents were in the front row. The thought of it now makes me feel faint, it's the most embarrassing thing that's ever happened to me in my life. The next day (AFTER MY PARENTS HAD WATCHED IT) the director decided we didn't need that part after all.

So it was only when we toured *Ghosted* that I got to go back on stage and I was terrified but excited at the same time. We really enjoyed the creative process of the show, which was ever evolving, and because Joanne had been touring non-stop for a few years, I knew that even if I got the worst stage fright ever, she could fill in. Luckily, that didn't happen but some nights, because the adrenaline is so high, it can almost feel like it's not happening when you're up on a stage in front of so many people. We had an amazing director, Una McKevitt, who I loved working with, so much so that I dragged her on board to help me edit this book. When you find somebody who inspires you and wants to create things as much as you do it's always good to cling onto them.

We played some really big stages during *Ghosted* and sometimes the inevitable would happen and I'd feel imposter syndrome coming on badly, thinking: 'Why am I up here in front of all these people?' But that can happen to me with so many different jobs. Why I don't know. It's not because I feel like I don't deserve it; I've worked really hard to get there my entire adult life, but it can all feel surreal at times. We toured for nearly two years with the show and although it was a lot of fun it could be hard at times. Most days I was tired because as well as working on the live show I still had to keep up with all of my other jobs and be around for the kids. Still, it is really crazy to think of the stages we were on and the amazing people who came to the shows. I'll never forget that.

While I really enjoy podding, two of my pods don't take any breaks throughout the year so I only get time off at Christmas when we release the 'best of' episodes. It can feel like a lot, but again I'm doing something I love so I should stop whinging. It's one of my favourite mediums to work on because you get involved in everything: the research, the edit, plus you control what goes out. We have amazing producers too; they just understand us and know how much I love getting to work on every aspect of it. Joe is our producer on *Ghosted*, Imo produces my other two pods and Pete helps with research, which is invaluable when you do three pods. We send in what we want to discuss and he helps us expand on it.

They will then sit through our record and send us our edits, which I then listen back to in case they've missed anything I really wanted included or if I want to move anything around. Sometimes it's hard to find the time to listen back to all three of the pods before they air so I do it at very random times and places. One time, when we were on tour with *Ghosted*, I listened to a recording of the latest episode of *Spencer and Vogue* in the hotel spa. Without even thinking I played it out loud in the mindfulness room at the spa because I didn't have my ear pods with me. It was only when a guest started singing an Irish ballad in protest that I noticed how annoying I was being. Joe and Una, who were lying on beds either side of me, still class that as one of the more unforgettable moments of their lives. I just saw it as killing two birds with one stone.

In September 2024 I started a new podcast *Never Live It Down*, interviewing really funny people and asking them questions they wouldn't always be asked. This pod requires something a little different as I'm hosting it on my own with a different guest each episode. For each episode I deep-dive each guest in advance and then we tailor that interview to what we think would help them open up more. It's a really fun part of the process for me and while I do have a guide of questions to lean on, the conversation totally depends on the guest. I'm naturally very nosy so I don't find it hard to go off on tangents. With podcasting I feel like I could keep it going for a very long time – I do assess things like that now I'm getting older. Some of the jobs I was doing ten years ago I can't do now and the same will apply in another ten years. Me at a roller disco promoting a brand? I'm not so sure I'll feel like doing that when I'm fifty, but I guess you never know.

One thing I don't understand is that there's quite a hatred for influencers. Why? It's just a job. When I started nobody was being paid to create content, but I was always trying to figure out a way to make money doing things I loved doing; for me it's about sticking to things I'm interested in and working around them. Years ago I wrote a fashion blog, which got picked up by *Hello!* magazine and even though I didn't make money off it I was on the *Hello!* website making connections with brands who wanted to be featured. Advertising has changed so much over the years and brands feel like they get a lot from influencers. It takes a lot of time, thought and effort to create the content they need.

While I don't remember the first time I made money from Instagram I do remember my first free gift. The thrill will never leave me! A jewellery brand called Katie Mullally sent me a gold twenty pence Irish coin. I loved it and I couldn't believe someone had given me something so valuable for free. A few years later I ended up creating a collection with Katie. If you are thinking of doing something along these lines, don't be disheartened when you aren't making much money at the start – nobody does. I can't stress enough how much work has to be done for free at the beginning of a career like mine. Even now, I will still take on very low-paid jobs because they are fun and could lead onto other opportunities.

Recently, I have started to take on fewer brands and focus on more long-term partnerships. I have worked with Fairy for many years, I'm the click clack mom in their ads – they used to have a plastic box that had two clicks when you closed it so you knew it was secure and out of reach of children (who tend to put things in their mouths). My tag line was 'Close the box with a click clack,' hence I became the click clack mom! (Now they're recyclable, so it's just a click.) The ads are on a lot and they have landed themselves a spot on French and German TV. They dub over my voice, so finally I speak French! I did take French lessons for a while and I loved my teacher, but at one point I wondered if the French were taking the piss. In French the same-sounding word means *green*, *towards*, *worm* and *glass*, depending on how you spell it – all too confusing for me, although I am still very attracted to the language. Spenno speaks fluent French and I have noticed that whenever we fight he suddenly has to call someone in France.

Nowadays the only thing important to me about my career is that I am successful and enjoying what I do. The fame aspect does not enter my mind any more, but it's not the same for everyone. I know someone who openly says they would rather be famous than successful and they do the strangest jobs, not for money but for attention, so that people will think they are brilliant. Wanting celebrity just for the sake of it is where so many people go wrong. I'm not a fan of the word 'celebrity' and don't consider myself one. The only people I really consider celebs are the ones in the movies, the people that you can't help but stare at if you ever spot them out because they exude an otherworldly quality.

Some aspects of my job can look super glamorous and sometimes I get to host awards shows and walk red carpets but, honestly, if you haven't been to one, trust me, they are not as glam as you'd think. Of course you have the nice prep side of things, like getting your hair and make-up done and wearing a beautiful dress, but in reality, I always feel like I'm in a rush and it doesn't feel as chilled as I would like with three kids running around. (Note to self, a make-up room in my dream house is essential.) On Insta I see people who have organised videographers to catch everything they do and I just don't understand: a) How can they be arsed? and b) How do they have the time? My Instagram would be more aesthetically pleasing if I put in a bit more effort instead of standing in front of the door handle in my kitchen trying to hide it for my outfit pics. (Also, note to self: find a white wall with no door handles for pictures.)

Truthfully, I don't enjoy red carpets at all. They're very embarrassing – like walking down the aisle on your wedding day. I always worry that the photographers won't want to take my picture and I'll be mortified, or I'll walk up to do press and the presenter will turn around and say, 'Oh, no thanks.' That does happen by the way; I have been interviewing people on the carpet and a producer will say to me 'Not them', which means you're supposed to try and avoid eye contact. There have been a few occasions where I have interviewed people anyway, knowing it won't be used, because it saves a lot of embarrassment for both of us and guilt for me. Being up for a BAFTA must be fun, but if you're not up for a BAFTA the show lasts five hours and you can't eat or drink or even doomscroll on your phone as it's televised. (Although the people-watching is absolutely glorious.)

I've had mainly good experiences in the industry and have made some really great friends through work but I do try to avoid the celebs. One 'celeb' I couldn't avoid working with was so rude to people that it made me cringe. He was so bad I actually had to say to him: 'Just stop being a wanker, nobody appreciates it.' It didn't work and I haven't seen him on TV in a long time. Fame goes to a lot of people's heads and that's when you know they're fucked. As soon as you start thinking you're better than someone else it's game over. A commissioner for a huge network once told me about a guy who was presenting a very high-end show and who was a complete wanker to him when he was starting out as a runner. When he then became a commissioner that same presenter was somewhat less successful and looking for work – the commissioner told him to go and shite.

People remember you when you're awful to them and being awful to someone doesn't make you have more power. When I was younger I worked in an Italian restaurant in Dublin, which I begrudgingly still go to because the food is so delicious (which matters more to me than holding a grudge). Anyway, the owner of the restaurant was so horrible to me and still to this day when I am dragged into that restaurant by my stomach I feel a sense of rage that I just can't let go of.

My approach to this industry and the people I work with is very simple. I want to enjoy each job I do and I want to have a nice, straightforward working relationship with people. Sometimes I make friends on jobs but they rarely tend to be the talent, although I've met lots of celebs that have been super nice: Claudia Winkleman was such a laugh and Graham Norton was as sound as you would expect. Spen and I have met a few actors at Glastonbury who were really cool too. Jamie Dornan was very down to earth and normal, funny as well. Rami Malek was very chill and sat with us for a while. We tried to play it cool and when he left we were just like ... what was that!

With celebrity friendships there can be something that's not quite true about them because there is so much competitiveness in this industry. I once went for lunch with three girls that were on a TV show together and it was like they all hated each other. If one went to the toilet the other two started laying into her and on and on it went, to the point that I was scared to go to the loo because God knows what they would say about me. I didn't bother with them after that. Imagine that was your group of friends. If they weren't in this industry and weren't after each other's jobs, maybe they'd have been nicer to each other? Who knows?

Rejection is a big part of this job and my favourite saying is 'what's for you won't pass you by', mostly because I had a huge amount of people getting work over me when I first started. I still do lose out on jobs, but I find it easier now than I did back then although some jobs are very tough to miss out on, especially when you want them so badly. I went for the hosting job on *Big Brother* one year and lost out to a really cool girl but that would have been a deadly job to get.

For a few years I had a manager called Max and although he doesn't manage me any more he very much took control of my career and we pushed forward together. He is a workhorse and I like to work so the relationship was great from the start. He now owns his own management company and we're good friends: 'the piggies'. (We have called each other 'pig' from day one – I have a nickname after all!) I left the company he worked in to go to my current agency as I wanted to focus more on TV work and that's what they excel at. Sometimes, I do work on some jobs with Max and my current manager combined.

Louisa at Money Management will be my lifelong manager, although I probably shouldn't say that in case she gets too comfortable. She's had my back from day one and I say this because when I first tried to get on the books of the company I was turned down. The owner, Francis, said they didn't have space for me. There were much bigger names on their books so I kind of understood but also thought he could have given me a chance. Being on the books of a management company with clients who are more successful than I am is a bonus as far as I'm concerned, because any jobs they don't want could trickle down to me! A year or so went by and then I got an email from Louisa asking me to go in for a meeting at Money Management and the rest is history. Take that, Francis!

Workwise, I think I have really found my way. Over the years there have been so many times where I didn't stick up for myself or realise my worth but I've since learned how important it is to always have your own back because if you don't, there might just be someone waiting there to stab you in it if you're not careful. At times I've worked with people who felt they were in competition with me, something I didn't even know about until much later, but that kind of information always has a way of being found out. If you're a shady person you will get caught out. I have had to grow a thicker skin and have my ear to the ground a lot more because unfortunately there will be people you can't trust.

I only like to work with people that are easy to work with, which I'm sure rings true for everyone but it's not just for me that that's important, it's for my management company too. There have been one or two brands I didn't want to work with any more because they were so awful to the people in my manager's office. I get that people have bad days but there's just no need to be an asshole and if you are, I'd rather avoid working with you for everyone's sake.

I'm also very aware of how I conduct myself around people because being known as unprofessional or rude is my idea of hell. Generally, I enjoy the company of everyone I work with so it's not like I have to try that hard. I don't think what I do and being in the public eye has changed me at all because when you have the right people around you and continue to appreciate how lucky you are to do what you're doing you should stay sane. I'm also nowhere near the same bracket as someone like Mariah Carey where her life changed and, of course, she has changed because of the level of her fame.

The one thing that can be tough at times is the nastiness online. It's something that's out of my hands, but I have been on the receiving end of not only abuse but also pathetic rumours made up by some terrible people. These are just very unhappy people who can't have much going on for themselves if they have the time for that crap. In life I think it's good to remember that nobody owes you anything. (Unless you've lent them a few quid. Although saying that, I've learned you should avoid lending people money where possible because you always end up feeling like the problem when you eventually ask for it back.)

Chapter Eighteen

Forever Young

'This is life's ultimate cruelty. It offers us a taste of youth and vitality, and then it makes us witness our own decay.'
Lisle Von Rhuman, *Death Becomes Her*

I am a huge Goldie Hawn fan and grew up watching all her movies, taking an extra special shine to *Death Becomes Her*, probably because I am a beauty addict. I love all creams, serums, make-up and tweakments. If there's the potential to look better, I'm all over it. 'We would like to burn the top layer of your skin off, but you will look amazing in a week.' Okay, book me in! Women invented staying young and it actually annoys me now that men have jumped on the bandwagon. They're calling it biohacking so it seems cool, but we got there first, boys! The first thing I ever tried was that vampire facial that Kim Kardashian got. I love the Kardashians and I just wish those girlos would tell us what they have really had done so I can stop drinking the swampy green smoothies they say are responsible for their good skin. Even though I know it's all nonsense, something inside me keeps saying: 'Be more Kourtney, have a matcha latte already!'

The vampire facial involves having your blood taken out, spinning that blood in a machine and then having the plasma that sits at the top of the blood injected back into your face. All I know is that it's supposed to make you look younger. Did I notice anything? Not really … and I still don't really understand the science behind it but if it's good enough for Kim K, it's good enough for me. When I'm going in for a tweakment the more down-time involved the better. I usually find it hard to relax, but for some reason when I'm getting a facial I totally chill, although if they have the internet and I don't have to wear those weird goggles then I will be knee-deep in my phone. But when full surrender to the tweakment is required I'll totally chill and throw the odd nap in too. There's nothing like a nap you didn't even know you had; usually I'll wake myself up with a grunt and it's only when I check my fitness ring that I find out I've napped.

It's the greatest gift for a sleep-lover like me. If someone could buy me sleep it would be the ideal present. There is a godawful movie that Justin Timberlake was in called *In Time*. I have watched it numerous times because I used to be deeply in love with JT. The storyline is that people run out of time and die much like we do but in the world of the movie they can buy and swap time. If that was available here I would be the greediest little gremlin wanting to live for ever. My JT obsession was the first borderline stalker crush I'd ever had because I thought he was the biggest ride I had ever seen and would have done anything to be with him. He left my old crushes on Eric Cantona and Liam Gallagher dead in the water. Well, maybe not, but certainly on the back burner. They will always be the first two men I had posters of on my bedroom wall, which doesn't say too much for my taste in men – I was into bad boys from the age of eight.

I loved Justin Timberlake so much that when he was playing in Dublin, I booked tickets for every single night and so did my pal Ashley (we were willing to share Justin). We were around sixteen at the time and knew all the words to every song on *Justified* (great album). We had even started on the NSync bullshit just to try and satiate our Justin obsession. Now, I'm about to say something that might get me cancelled but I feel full honesty is required in this book ... I took Justin's side when he broke up with Britney. Horrifying behaviour and I haven't forgiven myself since. LEAVE BRITNEY ALONE. For ever! It was essential that we met Justin when he was in Ireland because how else was he going to fall in love and marry both myself and Ashely? To make sure it happened I had a cunning plan. There was a very famous radio DJ in Ireland called Gerry Ryan and I pretended to be his assistant. I called up the local hotspot, Lillie's Bordello, where all the celebs were seen in Dublin and managed to book a table for Gerry Ryan's daughters, which on the night would be us.

Off we trotted to the concert, blissfully happy that we were about to lose our virginity to Justin Timberlake. We went straight to Lillie's after the concert and waltzed in pretending to be related to Gerry. We managed to get a great table and free drinks, can you imagine? Now, if Gerry's daughters ever get wind of this … Look, I was young and I simply can't apologise for what was the right thing to do in that situation. We got balubas drunk and Justin never showed up. I thought my heart may never recover. For the record I don't fancy him any more. The beatboxing finished him off.

Profhilo was and is one of my go-to treatments; you get a load of needles around your face, around eight I think, and they sting like nobody's business. Needles are something I have zero fear of, I love them. They are the givers of youth in my eyes. After Profhilo you are left with a dewy, glowy complexion a few weeks later. I would describe it as a layer of honey (hyaluronic acid) spreading under your skin. I once got it in my hands, which was a mistake and I had these fat little paws that wouldn't go down for weeks. They certainly didn't look any younger once the swelling went down either. I don't really like my hands; they could do with all the help they can get. Big meat cleaver hands that my friends in school used to slag me about all the time. I always wanted to be shorter with smaller hands and feet because it's considered more feminine. I guess I still do want to be like that, but you always want what you can't have and I'll surely shave a few inches off my height by the time I'm eighty; we all start shrinking by then, right?

As well as my big meat cleaver hands I have a very deep voice. If I ever call a takeaway or room service in a hotel they will always end with 'Is that everything, sir?' I've learned to just go along with it now to save both of us the embarrassment. When I filmed documentaries in Ireland, I presented one called *Transgender* with trans people and it was about trying to educate people on the trans community. As part of the job I got to do some really cool things, one of which was going to a trans convention in America. We were being shown around by one of the delegates who was so sound and informative and halfway through our conversation he asked me where I was on my transition journey. When I told him that I wasn't on that kind of journey I have never felt more boring in my life!

Botox. The word makes my heart skip a beat! I have never said I haven't had Botox but I've never confirmed it either; I assumed my line-free forehead did that for me. The good reason I have for never having confirmed or denied having it is because I despise the judgement made on people who decide to age disgracefully, which is my chosen path. Secretly I have been getting it for quite some time but used the excuse of 'Oh, I just got my brows done,' which threw people off the scent. This book is my coming-out party. I get Botox and I won't have a bad word said about it! Hiding it should have been very low on my list of priorities but when a woman in the public eye gets Botox that's all the press will ever talk about. Can you imagine if Michelle Obama came out and said she got Botox? No matter what else she did, every single headline would have to include Botox.

Michelle Obama and her freshly Botoxed face cures world hunger.

Michelle Obama and her line-free face after Botox create world peace.

It would be never bloody ending. So yes, I have had Botox and no, it wasn't my eyebrows.

By the time I need a facelift I'm hoping they'll have invented one where you don't need an operation. Although I did think they would have figured out a way to exercise in your sleep by now, and we'd have flying cars, so it may never be the case and if not, big decisions will have to be made. A facelift for my fifty-fifth, that has a nice ring to it. I know a woman in her eighties who had a facelift and she's going to have to take her ID to heaven because she looks so good.

I'm all for people who want to age whatever way they choose and I don't think there's an issue if someone wants surgery. I don't really care what anyone wants to do to themselves as long as it makes them happy. I am not the happiness police and I would never give my opinion on how other people choose to live their lives. I'd probably have a word with a few of the dictators, but outside of them, work away.

For most of last year I toyed with the idea of getting a boob job but I just don't like the idea of an operation. I found the knee operation I had after I hurt myself on *The Jump* very difficult to recover from. I hated going under, hated the painkillers and I felt like crap, so I'm in no rush to repeat that experience. For a short time in my teens I had big boobs and I have no idea where they went, they were probably sick of listening to me and legged it. Amber has enormous tatas, more than she would ever need, the greedy bitch, and I was left with the scraps. Mine are more similar to pecs but when I was younger I did have a way around the pecs and that was to wear the most padded bras I could find. When I took them off they would go THUD on the floor. They gave a good boob though, and still do – I have a couple in my drawer and my boobs are nearly up to my chin when I put them on.

One of my friends had a boob job; her boobs look amazing and after the operation she was back to work in two days. I always say do whatever makes you feel better, as long as you're not annoying anyone else, who gives a shit? My sad little droopy nips could do with a bit of love but after a long talk to myself I decided against it. I would still love bigger boobs but I'm self-conscious in a bikini and I would still be self-conscious in one with new boobs because I would then be worrying about the scars being on show. It's back to the double padded bras for me and on a Saturday night out on the town, I'll pop my trusty chicken fillets in – wham bam, thank you, mam, I have the biggest boobies in the room!

Other treatments I've tried on my quest so far: the salmon sperm facial. I would highly recommend it, it's great for the under eyes. I have had dark circles since I was a child and they don't bother me much but they seem to really annoy any skin doctors I go to. On hangover days I do look like I've been punched and I have to wear concealer so as not to scare people. In school one day the nuns were convinced I'd broken my nose because my eyes were so black. No matter what I do the panda eyes refuse to leave me so I've grown to love them, along with my moley moley moleys.

At this point I've lost count of the number of times people have asked if I would get the mole on my face removed. It's never anyone I know by the way, because that would be a right wanker thing to do. My brother used to love asking if I'd had Coco Pops for breakfast because they were all over my face. Theodore, my gorgeous, sweet, kind T, is absolutely terrified he will end up with a mole like mine because he's asked me quite a few times if one would grow on his face, how I got mine and how could he stop himself getting one. It's lucky I don't take offence too easily, although I could have done without that moley lad (The Mole) on Austin Powers because I did get called Moley Moley Mole for quite some time after that.

Besides permanently trying to make myself look younger and fake tanning all the time, I think I am fairly low maintenance. On the rare occasion I have my nails done I feel like I've made the biggest effort in the world. I am always jealous of other people's nails, especially the fancy nail art ones, but not one part of me would be able to sit down for that long very often. My attention span is close to zero at times and certainly when getting my nails done, so it's a very special treat. Tanning is essential, it makes me feel so much better about myself when I have a tan and I own a business that sells it so I will never be without it. My pal Kieran and I connected over our mutual love of tan and together we created Bare By Vogue. On holidays I used to always burn myself to a crisp trying to get the perfect tan, olive oil being my SPF of choice, but at sixteen I started using fake tan and ever since I don't remember a time where I haven't had it on my body. Irish people in general love having a tan, we are one of the biggest consumers of tan in the world so what better place to start a tan brand? (Although there is an urban myth going around the Bare By Vogue offices in Cork that I, in fact, have never worn tan.) Blasphemy. Without a layer of tan I just don't feel like myself and I know that seems incredibly shallow, but I've been wearing it for so long it feels like a second skin.

Owning my own tanning brand had never occurred to me and at the time I doubt I would have had the courage to do it – or the business know-how. Kieran popped into my life at the perfect time and he's taught me a huge amount. When it started selling well I met the owner of Dunnes Stores (a huge department store in Ireland) on holiday. Never one to miss an opportunity, I jumped at the chance to try and get it onto the shelves in Dunnes. It was only when she asked me my business partner's name that I realised I didn't know it. Two years of knowing Kiki and I didn't know his second name; he was just on my phone as 'Kieran Tan'. (I've left him in my phone with that name. I prefer it.) Supposedly Kieran is a dying name so I asked his parents, and they gave me their blessing to rename him Kiki Tan.

In terms of ageing, one thing I have some fear about is being perimenopausal because it just sounds horrific. I keep hearing horror stories about anxiety being a side effect and I really don't need my anxiety to get any worse than it already is. Getting older worries me too, even though I should be happy about it because the alternative is being dead. Sure, aren't you lucky you're not dead! There I am worrying about things that don't yet affect me, but at least I'm calling myself out about it. Hopefully my therapist sees this and congratulates me on my progress. (I'm not sure my therapist has ever seen progress in me but I do tend to make him laugh, although I'm not sure if that's a good or a bad thing.) At times I see progress in myself and I know I'm doing some good work when my anxiety is under control, but as soon as I feel anxious I give my therapist a call; thank God it's on Zoom so I don't have to leave my house. If I prioritised it a bit more I might see more results, but I don't want to be over ther-apised – mostly I like to get on with it rather than dwell on the shitty things too much, so I Band-Aid quite a lot.

One thing I'll always worry about is my health. Watching my dad go in and out of hospital over the years has left a lasting mark on me. It's why I fret about drink-ing so much and beat myself up after a night out, even though it's such a rare experience these days. Something I really had to get on top of lately was my vaping habit. Vaping is absolutely disgusting. That's what I have to keep telling myself because there was a period of time where not a day went by that I didn't have a blue-razz-flavoured vape hanging out of my mouth. It's actually mind-blowing how addictive they are. When I have a drink I could be partial to a cig or two but I wanted to stop that and decided vaping would be a better option so I took one on a night out and that was that. Couldn't stop myself. I'd fall asleep with it in my hand, wake up and start vaping. Then when I did have a drink, I'd have a cigarette in one hand and a vape in the other! Madness. When I started to hear a popping in my throat it really freaked me out and I would tell Spen I had given up and feel like a complete idiot when he'd catch me red-handed sneaking a puff. Many times I tried and failed to quit solo but the draw of the stunning blue razz was too much; I succumbed time and again.

Finally, I had to call in the big guns, a hypnotist. Usually I find those things to be a load of wank but desperate times call for desperate measures. The session was on Zoom so regardless of what happened, there would be minimum time wasted. Halfway through being hypnotised my three kids stormed into our room. (That's another thing for the next house, a hidden room!) The hypnotist put me back under and within an hour we were all done and I haven't touched a vape since. It must have had something to do with that (plus a little self-restraint too), but I honestly never thought I'd be without one of those in my pocket. Good timing too, as they are about to ban them! I know people who get through three vapes a day; at the equivalent of thirty cigarettes a day, that's a pretty hefty toll on your lungs. Thankfully, they're pretty adept at recovery. I'll still have the odd cig when I have a drink, but it's so seldom the doctor told me it doesn't matter.

Chapter Nineteen

Trust

I'm forty on my next birthday. FORTY. How did that happen? When I was in my twenties I used to look at thirty-year-olds and think they looked so old and battered, but maybe they hadn't yet discovered Botox. I thought I would be terrified of turning forty, but with age comes acceptance and a little bit of wisdom. (I will never accept anxiety; it's the worst thing about me but everything else I more or less accept.) I'm happy with myself and my life and if I died tomorrow (touch wood) I would honestly think: 'What fun that was.' Saying that, I do not want to die tomorrow. Some people (Spen) think they'd like to peg it at eighty but not me, I'd stick around for ever if I could, although it'd be just my luck that they'll invent some kind of pill that extends your life just as I bite the dust. I hope not though, because believe me I will be the first in line for that pill.

Every year I go in and out of caring about my birthday, ranging from going all out over the top to trying to avoid people knowing it's my big day. I don't remember many of my birthdays or parties as a kid although there is evidence of them so I can't even call Sandra out on it. The last one I properly remember is my eighteenth, which I threw myself. My best pal at the time helped me organise it (I'd been kicked out of my house for good reason and was living with my dad). We had a menu of booze and chicken dippers, which were all I ever really cooked at the time besides some WeightWatchers soup a pal of mine told me about that was totally revolting and had no place on a birthday menu.

Even though I love attention, for some reason the attention around my birthday I've never enjoyed as much. The multiple texts can feel like a lot of admin on a day you're meant to be doing nothing. I know I sound awful and if I didn't get the texts I would be raging, or if Amber didn't make me a collage for Instagram I would think I'd done something wrong. Still, there's no chance of me reposting it because I hate when people repost birthday messages, which is a bit mean of me because people should be allowed to enjoy the day as they please.

My thirty-eighth birthday was one of those times when I went all out and took eight of my good pals to a country house for the weekend. I organised all the shopping and booze and brought it all down so nobody had to do a thing. Well, they were meant to do ONE thing, the only thing I couldn't organise myself! I had had a beautiful cake made and couldn't wait to eat it but nobody bothered to put candles in it and sing me 'Happy Birthday' – not one single person the whole weekend. It was a big cake! You couldn't miss it but they did!

The place we were staying at even sent a cake to the house and everyone dived into it, but again, not a note of the famous song. We kicked the absolute shite out of ourselves with booze that weekend so I'm assuming everyone was either too drunk or too hungover to remember. I didn't say anything because you can't ask your friends to sing 'Happy Birthday' to you; it's too pathetic. Also, I assumed they would remember to do it eventually. It was only when we were getting ready to leave and packing up the cake that I finally accepted: it's not happening. After that weekend I did think I wouldn't bother with a birthday party again. That is until I was in Italy for my thirty-ninth birthday and the hotel very kindly made a massive fuss of me and I realised how much I loved it; why shouldn't I get treated on my special day?

Spencer and I had decided to go for a run that morning before breakfast and, as always, he was off to do 20k plus because he's a total weirdo, but I only wanted to do 7k. The plan was I'd have breakfast alone, meet him for a swim and then fly back to the kids who would be heartbroken to miss a birthday and a rainbow cake. When

I arrived at breakfast the hotel had set up a table with rose petals and a big heart-shaped trellis! I never mind eating alone because I'll always have my phone but I was very embarrassed when I saw the trouble they had gone to. In the end though, I had a very romantic breakfast alone, which I really enjoyed. It made me think that for every birthday going forward I should do something to mark it, and so should you if you're birthday averse like me. Even if it's having cake with your dog, do something to mark it.

I'm not sure what I'm going to do to mark my big birthday but I will probably do a few small things with my favourite people, or maybe I'll get Pitbull to come and do a concert in my back garden and invite everyone I know. When I was younger I imagined forty-year-olds as having dentures and walking sticks. So far, I have neither of those things; a couple of veneers, but I have gotten to forty relatively unscathed. I feel at a good place in my life, doing a job I love and having a great gang of pals and a family I adore. It's a good spot to be in. I think if you're happy then you're successful and my friends make me endlessly happy. What I love about good friends is you can call them, say a quick hello and rant away about something that's annoyed you, then quickly say goodbye having righted all the wrongs in the world. And let's be honest, your pal will always take your side if they are a good one.

Still, I firmly believe in a cut-off point in certain conversations. If you're helping a friend through a break-up you will always come to a point where you simply can't take any more of the same conversation going around and around in circles. A friend of mine went through a difficult break-up and I was there for her, of course, but after around three months I could feel the energy drain from me when she started up the same conversation. When I told her I was pregnant she said, 'Aw, that's nice,' and went straight back into her usual rant. Sure, I know I'm pregnant most of the time but surely it's still a special slice of information? We all do it, though. When I went through my divorce one of my pals had to say in the nicest way possible that she couldn't hear me go on about it any more. It was the kick up the arse that I needed.

By your late thirties you more or less have your solid friendships. I have had a few very sound people sneak up on me and I've let them in but I lost a few others so I'm on an even keel. These days I am more protective of who I let into my life and not just because I work in an industry where people's intentions aren't always good, but because I've had a few bad experiences with people over the years. Mostly, I'll give everyone the benefit of the doubt and trust them until they give me a reason not to, but it's easy enough to figure people out. If you watch how people interact with other people, it will tell you a lot about them. One thing I really don't like is someone being rude to someone else. I know that you can be in a bad mood sometimes and not be yourself but it's different with people who are repeat offenders. I like to be generous – super generous if I can – but it bothers me when people expect it. I love sharing but I hate being asked! I know how lucky I am to get sent products by companies who are promoting them and I have a huge amount of make-up that I can't possibly use all by myself. Whenever anyone comes over I ask them if they want to go and go choose five things but I immediately leave the room because if I stay I might think, 'Actually, I might wear that orange lipstick one day, give it back!'

I have lost a couple of friendships over the years, but that's just a part of life although, obviously, unfortunate. One of my very best friends broke away from our group of friends at home a few years ago. She was one of my best friends for all my teenage years and into my thirties, so at the time it was a big blow and I couldn't understand why it had happened. To this day I still don't know why but it feels that was meant to happen, a loss but in the long run it was for the best. There have been two occasions where people I knew, one I was very close to, threatened my career. There was a suggestion that they might discuss private things in my life with the press and that is a tough pill to swallow. It's a really low dig and for me a complete line in the sand; there's absolutely no way back from that. Also scarlet for them because realistically the press wouldn't care – I'm not Cher!

Another friendship I've lost was after they lashed out at me one too many times. One of these times was at a work event and it was around hundreds of people. It was so bad and I was mortified – a friend screaming at me for something someone else had said. They were very drunk so I was just trying to ignore it because I had worked hard for months on that job, hours and hours a day, up at the crack of dawn every morning. What was meant to be a fun day was totally ruined. They were going through a difficult time so although we don't hang out any more, I still really like that person and would love to see them again.

Another fall out wasn't with a friend of mine but with a friend of Spencer's. From early on I had my reservations about them and got the feeling I couldn't trust them. It wasn't long before they showed their true colours and although I wouldn't ignore them if I saw them again, I'd steer well clear.

I don't know if it's an age thing, but even the people I am no longer friends with, I still want them to do well, there is really no animosity on my part, for sure. If I saw them I would genuinely be happy to bump into them; just because you aren't friends doesn't mean you have to hate that person. It's also impossible to hang on to every friend you make because how on earth could you hang out with that many people? It's very natural to shed friends as you get older and you change as a person. It's really sad and very unfortunate but it's important to always surround yourself with supportive and kind people. Even in the last few years I have seen a different side to people I thought were lifelong friends of myself and Spencer. It's not that I expect a friend to be perfect at all times because that's just not how life is – I can be annoying at times, everyone can – but I always want to be a good friend to people, and to me that means being their cheerleader instead of tearing them down. There have been situations where damage was purposefully caused to myself and Spen and that is something I can't ever get past. If you are trying to bring down either of us you are essentially trying to hurt our family, and that is what is most important to me.

In this industry you will have people that you think are your friends, and when they do something that is so disloyal, they break your trust completely and leave you questioning their motives. Why try to be a friend when behind your back they're trying to cause trouble for you so as to protect themselves? It's deeply upsetting when that happens and, if I'm really honest, it makes you incredibly paranoid. The first time it happened to me was the first time I think I ever experienced any kind of depression. For months I found every day really difficult; I couldn't sleep well and I just felt sad all the time. I feel sad now when I think about it, because I really don't ever want to be in a place like that again. One of the worst things about it was that it was all down to things I couldn't control, so I was unsure of how to get myself out of it. But I did, and I learned to be more guarded. I still read things in the papers from a 'source' and I have my suspicions of who that might be. I'll never truly know unless I pull a Coleen Rooney, but if you even have to wonder about that kind of thing you know there isn't a real friendship there.

Spencer and I like doing the same things so we never fight over what to do; we just enjoy being in each other's company. At the same time I think it's essential to have your own group of friends outside your relationship. You need friends that are totally yours. If you don't have your own pals and something goes wrong, you could lose them in the break-up, so I like to err on the side of caution. My friends are way sounder than Spen's are so he's usually trying to steal mine. Sometimes, I'll remind Spencer that if anything were ever to happen and we broke up, he isn't keeping my brother Alexander, my cousin Cillian or my best pal Kieran, all of whom he has become very close to.

Not only is Cillian great craic, he's also been there for me (and Spen) during very difficult times and is just an all-round brilliant person. He always makes a real effort with our kids, which I commend him for because most people stay away between the kids' waking hours of 7 a.m. and 7 p.m. He lives in London, which is great for us because it's nice to have some family around. The Irish are notorious for seeking each other out in foreign lands (not that London is so foreign, but you get what I mean). Irish people go away on holidays looking for Irish bars so we can find more Irish people.

These days I am always trying to get friends to come running with me or go for a nice walk because getting two things done at once is a personal favourite of mine. Exercise with pals is the ultimate duo: great conversation and you'll feel amazing at the end of it. My anxiety around health pushes me to train too. If you're forty or over, weight training is one of the best things you can do for your body. Someone once told me that you get really old and battered from running, that it pulls your face down. As I don't need extra sag and (as mentioned) tend to believe everything I'm told, I did stop running for a while. Then I read it was fine and doesn't age you so the runners went straight back on and out I went. The plan was to run and not harp on about it but I can't seem to stop myself, I've even got a disgusting-looking running watch so there's no going back for me. Running gives me the ability to do two things at once, like listen to music or a pod, which is a large part of why I love it. When I was in Amalfi I wouldn't have seen anything if I hadn't been running because the traffic was so awful. I did almost get hit by a bus or car on each run, but the views were worth it.

I had a weird but totally acceptable thought today: I must make some younger friends. As I intend on out-living all of mine I don't wanna be alone when I'm old, and so I'll have a better chance of avoiding that with friends half my age. No matter what, I'm always forward planning. When you get above a certain age you become friends with people of all ages. My aunts Jeana and Naomi are such good pals of ours. When I say ours, I mean myself and Ambi, because we always feel like a team! Jeana lives in Oxford and is like my bonus mom in England. When we were younger and had no money we would go and stay in Jeana's and she would take us shopping to the outlets, and always get us a Chinese takeaway. Then she would give us each a bucket of ice and whatever booze we wanted and we would sit there watching TV and talking absolute shite. I've woken up many times on Jeana's couch, the sign of a great night – she bored me to sleep! Jeana is a permanent holiday buddy of ours. We love when she comes on holiday with us and not just because she's the ultimate help with our kids, it's because she is the most fun ever.

My aunt, Naomi, who taught me in school and has managed to forgive me of my sins, is another constant in my life and someone I see as a very good friend. She's a much nicer person than the rest of us, bar the aforementioned regifting, which brings her down a bit, but now I don't even get annoyed about it; I just think good on her.

Once I gave her a gorgeous, very expensive handbag. I did find it unusual that I hadn't seen her parading around with it and showing off to the highest degree, but she had raffled it off in the golf club. What a witch. Whenever I'm home in Howth I love going on walks with her because I don't even have to open my mouth and she tells me everything that's been going on. I even ran 5k with her on the phone one day and didn't open my mouth once, she's like a podcast.

When I was younger she was always sliding me twenty euros and I will never forget that because when you really want to go out with your mates and someone gives you a free twenty euro it's a real life raft. (I bumped into one of my dad's friends, Seamus, when I was around twenty and he slipped me a fifty. I was way too old to be accepting cash gifts, but I still snatched the hand off Seamus. If someone handed me a fifty tomorrow I'd probably accept it.) Naomi was also a superstar during all my break-ups; her way of making me feel better was to take me shopping for new bras and knickers – not sure why, as there was nobody to show them off to!

Chapter Twenty

Keeping Up With The Wilsons

Growing up you never imagine your parents being your friends, and although there are still boundaries of sorts you do become friends. It happened later with my mom than it did with my dad. The transition was harder because my mom and Neil would always be stricter, for instance I wouldn't swear in front of Neil even today; there is that line I just wouldn't cross.

My cousins, all over the age of thirty, will go and chill in their mom's bed for naps and to watch TV and that fascinates me, because that's never been my relationship with mom. But while we may not have been the best of friends in the past, I know for a fact that I'm her favourite now. It took a while but I have flown up the ranks with a lot of hard work and determination! This is no mean feat, considering she used to call Alexander 'Ray' (as in a 'ray of sunshine'). Someone pass me a bucket, I don't remember him hoovering the stairs! Sandra and I talk all the time and I always want to be around her, but I go by the three-day rule with her and Neil; they love you, love you, love you until it hits day three and then you are invading their space and in the war zone. EVACUATE.

Sandra puts an outfit together extremely well and has quite a big following on Instagram, almost fifty thousand. Her username is @sandrawilson3614 (I would be disowned if I didn't give her Insta a shout out). She always has a glass of champagne to celebrate a big hike in followers so let's get her deranged. One of her favourite things to do is to tell everyone how many followers she has (it has to be said, it is quite impressive). It's all fashion on her page and I do end up swiping a lot of what she posts; she's basically working for Zara for free because that's mainly what her clothes posts consist of. My mom's life is very relaxing (which is well deserved after raising four kids) and I aspire to it when I'm older, but at the same time I just can't ever see myself as a relaxer.

She's a really good grandmother but she taps out a lot quicker than Spencer's mom would. On a recent visit to London she came over for a couple of hours and then she was ready to go home and chill in a child-free environment. She told me recently she left because she knew dinnertime was imminent. Personally I would never judge anyone for escaping dinnertime with kids. If people want to call in around that time, I will always give them a warning of what to expect. Spen's mom, on the other hand, will come over, clean our house and stay with the kids until bedtime. She even has them for sleepovers but my mom prefers doing shorter stints. I might be the same.

For a while Rico was my least favourite sibling, but now it's a pendulum between himself and Alzo as to who's my favourite. He's a brilliant dad and is the only one in the family that can compete with me on the decoration front, although when I saw his recent Halloween decorations they didn't look as good as they did in the picture so I think I am still queen of decorations. When I go home to Howth, I really love hanging out with him and his family. He has three kids and our kids love them, so it's perfect. His son and T do go around battering each other but at the same time they are the best of friends. Their daughter Jeanie is my sweet angel face and was my first ever niece, so I'm obsessed with her. She's got spice – I took her shopping for her birthday once, a huge mistake. She cost me a bomb, but I admired her ability to get the very most out of me, clever girl.

Fred has a very strange habit of tasting plain rice when his order of Chinese food arrives and I don't know why Amber and I are so horrified by that, but we are. His big order of delicious Chinese food arrives and he has this weird thing that he has to have a big spoonful of plain rice before trying anything else. Amber and I are sauce queens so this is totally rotten to us. We have sauce for our sauce and the butter on my toast has to have teeth marks in it when I take a bite – nothing dry gets past this big mouth.

Frederick is really funny and I can never take what he says as gospel because he is permanently taking the piss out of me. He'll make up an extravagant and awful lie about somebody and wait until I'm shocked to the core before he starts laughing at his own bullshit. Amber is violently gullible, even more than me, and I believe everything I'm told. I was once able to convince Amber that I was buying Shetland ponies for our balcony in London; she also believed me when I told her my son T was being charged for robbing from our local shop.

Although Alexander, or Alzo as we call him, is the youngest of us, he's more serious and mature than any of us ever were or currently are. He's his own man and would be happy to spend loads of time alone, but can also be very good fun when given a little shove. He thinks Amber and I are too wild so avoids us like the plague when we go out, or if he's forced to go out with us he leaves early or sneaks off to bed. He'll then spend the next day swanning around to show us how he's not hungover, whereas I spend the next day terrified I'm about to be bitten by the venomous pit viper that is a hungover Amber.

Alzo went to uni in Berkeley, California because he's an amazing golfer and got a scholarship or at least, I hope he did, and wasn't secretly spending my inheritance.

He tried living and working in Ireland when he came back but didn't enjoy it; Alzo went to secondary school in Edinburgh so Ireland holds no real connection for him besides us. I do try to get him to go back more but it just doesn't have the same pull as it does for me. When he moved to London Spen gave him a job at CleanCo, which wasn't his passion, but now he's found a job doing something he loves: mergers and acquisitions (I only remember that because of the film *American Psycho*). He loves his job so much and I'm so happy that he got to do that because he was starting to rot in Ireland.

Alzo lives with Spencer and me at the moment and we love having him with us – he's so chilled, so funny and just lovely to be around. Before he lived with us he lived in my parents' place in Ireland because they live in Spain. So Alzo lived alone in Howth, but because he had been endlessly looked after by my mother growing up, he could barely cook or wash his own clothes.

He did, however, learn how to make bolognese and make bolognese that boy did. He would make a huge amount every Sunday and have it for lunch and dinner the entire week. Can you bloody imagine eating that much bolognese for the guts of a year? He then moved onto fajitas and I was surprised he didn't turn into one. When he cuts up raw chicken he does it with a knife and fork because he can't stand the texture of it on his fingers;

it takes him a lifetime to get through one chicken breast but he perseveres, although it doesn't help that he washes his hands every five seconds.

Frederick and Alexander are brilliant but they're not Amber. A brother and sister relationship is very different, I think, to that of two sisters; one of the main reasons I'm considering having a fourth child is so I can, hopefully, give Gigi a sister. If I do have another child and it isn't a girl, I have to admit I would be sad for Gigi. Every baby is a miracle and I would love him madly if he were a boy, but a girl for Gigi is the dream. Having a sister has been brilliant for me.

Amber is the life and soul of the party and everyone feels happy to be in her company. The only time you don't want to be around her (or even in the same country) is the day after her hangover day. She is like a living nightmare that day. There have been times I've left Ireland and flown back to London early because Amber's post hangover mood was so rancid. You can do nothing right, and she will drag you to the depths of despair with her. It's not even just with people she knows: she will pull that with anyone, but when she is on form she is the dream. She's like Graham Norton: when she enters a room, everyone turns and desperately wants to hang out with her.

Actually, I think I might ditch Amber if Graham wanted to be friends with me, he's at the pinnacle of TV and a great writer – I love his books. There's been a couple of events where I've been desperate to say hi to him but just couldn't muster up the courage; around people I admire I can get very shy and what happens is I end up completely ignoring them. Our stars finally aligned and I got to work with him hosting a question panel with the contestants of his new show *LOL: Last One Laughing*. He was even better in real life. If he'd been awful I would have been devastated (that's happened to me with other well-known people who shall remain nameless)!

While we've always had a great relationship, Amber and I still row even now. Recently she stole a large bottle of very expensive shampoo from my shower as well as my charger from beside my bed. She refused to admit to either of them so I told her: 'You're in your forties now, Amber, and it's unacceptable to still be robbing from people. If that shampoo isn't where I left it when I get home I'll help myself to all those perfumes that you hide from me. I know where they are, Amber, I drowned myself in one this morning, sprayed at least £5 pounds worth all over me!' Of course, we both always think we're right when we fight but I'm much more stubborn than Amber so sometimes an argument can last a lot longer than it needs to.

There are times when I cry thinking about the fact that Amber will die (I know, I'm insane) but I love her so much. In Ancient Egypt some people were buried in tombs with their cats. I'll be Amber's cat when she dies.

Chapter Twenty-One

Death Becomes Her

There are two topics I could endlessly talk about and death is one of them. It's a certainty and to my complete shock and horror, there is absolutely no way of avoiding it. I know people say there are two certainties in life, taxes and death, but I know people who never paid tax in their lives – my dad, Freddie, for one. Whoops, I just ratted him out but he's hit the other certainty so I doubt the taxman is going to exhume his body and make him cough up. I will also get this checked in case I'm in some way liable to pay his taxes because I pay enough of my own and I'm not sorting him out.

Death is so strange. It's happening to all of us and we are just walking around like it's not. I cannot get my head around it. It was after my children were born that I became death-obsessed and I've heard that happens to a lot of people because we want to be around for our kids. While

I do like the odd break from them, death would just be slightly too long for me. On one of my faves Kim K's Instagram I read a quote that said, 'The sad part about motherhood is that you're raising the one person you can't live without to be able to live without you.' Spent quite a while crying over that and it really made me realise that my children being happy is the number one most important thing for me: I would sacrifice anything for them.

Whenever someone starts discussing a grandparent with me I find it amazing, as mine all died when I was quite young – but Nanny lived until she was in her eighties. My grandad died of a stroke and then my dad died of a stroke, which makes you wonder if that's your own destiny. When I was going through my very strange obsession with death, I could barely leave the house without worrying about someone, randomers, anyone that I thought was about to kick the bucket. Walking along the street I would spot an older man or woman and say: 'Jesus, they must be petrified.' Spen would say: 'Of what?' and I'd think it was quite clear they would be terrified of dying because they were so close to it. They could be perfectly fit and healthy but if they looked old that was it for them in my mind.

Spencer and I went for a very fancy meal in Scotts restaurant over in London and again I spotted an older gentleman and immediately felt sad for him. *Doom*, I thought! When in reality he was thrilled with himself, knocking back wine that was probably 100 quid a bottle and necking oysters like there was no tomorrow. Still, I thought, it's coming for you. Enjoy the oysters while you can, my friend. That's just how my mind worked at the time. Now I am way more chilled about it but I did need my therapist to help me with it as my thinking around death was becoming obsessive. I do still get the urge to ask people about it, like my mom who would also be slightly scared of dying. I'm only desperate to find out if she's scared but I'm stopping myself from asking so I don't freak her out. Sandra, if you're reading this, ARE YOU SCARED?

Control is something I love, it's a hobby of mine and death isn't something we can control, which I hate. I've read so many books around the topic that I don't put them on my bookshelf because people will think I'm more of a weirdo than I am. Basically I'm studying how to die, and to die well is something we all deserve. Our brains would survive for over 2,000 years but it's our bodies that fail us. If I could live for 2,000 years I would, although I wouldn't if I couldn't have my family and pals around me. Without getting too philosophical it really is very important who you spend your time with. As I get older I have dropped a lot of dead weight in terms of friendships, and it leads to a more fulfilling life.

Life after death is something I really believe in, it's the only thing that keeps me sane. *Many Lives Many Masters* by Dr Brian Weiss was quite a life-changing book for me. In it he all but confirmed that there was life after death and, to top it off, he said we stay with our group of souls we are on earth with, which brought me endless amounts of joy although maybe a few of the mediocre people will take a wrong turn! I did warn you that I believe everything I'm told and this made me feel a lot better about death, so I'm taking it. Lots of people think there is nothing after death but being positive about it makes more sense and certainly makes you feel less frightened.

I've come to terms with my death on many occasions, sometimes weekly and on rare occasions it could be twice in a day. It all happens when I fly because I convince myself that it's my time. I'm currently sitting quite happily on a plane thirty plus thousand feet in the air because I have survived another take off! Here's how it goes: I'm on the runway completely fine, the plane starts moving. I'm now not fine at all. We take off and I'm jumping around like someone who has no control over their limbs – and I spend the first ten minutes jumping around. Then I start taking deep breaths and I rationalise: you've had a lovely life and this will be quick, you won't even feel it. It will be a little scary going down and then bam! it's all done. You'll be grand.

Then we go above the clouds and that's when I know it's okay so I pop on some *Selling Sunset* and chill out for the rest of the flight, oblivious to the fact that I've scared the shite out of anyone who was unlucky enough to get the seat beside me. I once sat beside Joe, our producer on *My Therapist Ghosted Me,* on a flight into Knock in Ireland. The weather was appalling so this time around I was petrified of landing, almost belting him in the face every so often. The diverted landing nearly sent me over the edge and then I remembered this airport was built for the Pope's visit to Ireland, you surely can't get killed there. Luckily we didn't because the selection of sweets they have at that airport is outrageous.

I'm lucky enough to have not yet experienced (touch wood) a near-death experience but I love reading stories about people going into the white light. Spencer had a near-death experience that he counts. He was in a speed-boat and he fell out at high speed, dislocating both of his shoulders; he couldn't swim to the surface and thought that was the end for him. He has told me other stories that make me think he's like a cat – there has been more than one close shave for sure, nine-lives Matthews. Having your life flash in front of your eyes would bring perspective to most people, but Spencer is one of the few people who is very comfortable with the idea of death. He's not searching for it but he's not scared of it and considering he almost faced it, I tend to believe him.

My obsession with death extends to the afterlife so when I was asked to film a show in which we were going to the most haunted places in Ireland I jumped at the chance; I do some very weird jobs at times but I always choose them on the basis of loving the brand or the idea. As stupid as you might think this sounds I was almost positive I would see a ghost. I wanted proof, I wanted to see it with my own eyes and although I scared the absolute shite out of myself, I never caught a glimpse of a ghost. That isn't to say I now don't believe in them, I just think some people are more susceptible to that type of energy. I realise this is quite witchy woo, but now that we've all decided aliens exist can we not think the same for ghosts? Those poor bastards get ignored enough as it is. There is nothing better for me than watching a horror film, well more of a paranormal type job, and being so frightened I feel like I might just crawl out of my skin. I only watch them during the day now or my sleep is so badly affected by the thoughts of a ghost dragging me out of the bed.

I would like to end this chapter on a high note: the planning of my own funeral. I did a podcast with Kathy Burke, it's called *Where There's a Will, There's a Wake* and you essentially plan what you would like to happen at your funeral. Even in death you are still sorting shit out. It's a very funny pod and you can get some great ideas for your own wake! I've read about quite a few people who have had their own funerals before they died – they weren't just being random about it as they were very sick and I thought it was a great send-off for themselves. Why should you miss the party you'll be paying for? It would be lovely to hear all of the nice things said about you and you can make everyone cry with your own speech, truly unforgettable.

If I was to plan my own funeral, firstly, I would like to die on a Thursday. This will be a three-day affair all about me, myself and I. There won't be a dry eye in the house, such will be the devastation of the loss of Vogue, beloved mother, grandmother, wife, sister and friend. I would preferably die at home in my very comfortable bed to the sound of Dr Dre's *2001*: the album can play through as I like all of the songs but exiting the world on a Dre and Eminem track would be ideal. Now whoever is in charge please take in this next piece of information carefully. On the unusual circumstance that I have not pre-tanned (I might be tired on the account of me dying, so no judgement) I must be bronzed from top to toe, Bare by Vogue ultra dark instant please.

Then I would like a layer of illuminator on any body part that's showing. The nails must be done in a pillar-box red, Carla can do my hair and as Ashley is two weeks younger than me I can only assume she will still be around so I would like a daytime smoky eye with dewy skin. I do not want to meet whoever is up there looking like I've been dragged through a ditch. I'll go in gym gear, something chic that if you were going to lunch you could get away with, and maybe with an oversized blazer – comfort is key as God knows when the next time I change will be! Okay, onto the celebrations. On the Thursday I assume everyone will head out to have a toast to me, but I refuse to foot the bill for that; I'll cover the wake and the funeral. At the wake people will walk under two enormous Christmas trees (I am dying at the end of November because I love Christmas decorations). The house will look like you have just walked into the North Pole, everyone will be taking pictures of all of it because they simply cannot believe how beautiful the room looks, and Harrods will be totally mortified by their decorations that year which look shitty in comparison to mine.

I will be laid out in a room just off the main room propped up in all my glory with four professional wailers present at all times. My room will have a playlist of grime and rap, everyone gets five minutes with me to tell me how much they will miss me and then can head straight back out to the party, which will have turned into a semi rave by 9 p.m.

A few of my friends get kicked out because they're too deranged but the party ends by 11 p.m. so everyone can get some sleep before the festival that will be my funeral. I won't be sleeping on my own; the kids (who are adults by then) have put bunk beds in my death room to spend the night with me.

The big day arrives and I almost come back to life with the excitement of it all. Everyone arrives at my house for mimosas and straight champagne (personally I have never understood the orange juice part). I head off to the festival site around 12 with everyone following. It's chilly out so make sure to pop me into my ski suit, the all pink one will look great with my tan. We will have a very short ceremony, plenty of tears will be shed and then come the speeches. Because I want around eight to ten of them, halfway through there will be an interval with bacon sandwiches and cocktails.

After all of the speeches I would like to be walked back down the aisle to 'Freed from Desire' – everyone will need a good pick-me-up after the sadness of the funeral and, like I said earlier, that song always gets people going. A quick burial for me and I will be going on top of Amber – I'm the organised one and she won't have organised herself a plot when she died so I let her into mine. That actually happened with my dad: he was adamant he wouldn't be going into the ground on top of his parents so made my Aunty Sharon swear to him he could go in her plot, which is right beside their parents. Sharon was so worried he would be put in the wrong grave and come back to haunt her, something he might do (I don't get my grudge holding from nowhere) that she went up to check the morning of the funeral. All was good, thankfully. I would be happy to share a plot with Ambi but is it bad to say I would like to take the dogs with me too? Like the Egyptians did? I just really don't like being alone, but I will let my family make that call.

So after I am out of the way and enjoying myself watching from above the real fun will start. It is going to be a full day festival that finishes at 1 a.m. The headline act will be Daft Punk, although they may be like the Abba holograms at that point because, as far as I know, they are no spring chickens themselves. All my favourite DJs will perform throughout the day. Food trucks will be everywhere with my favourite food: wings, ribs and Irish Chinese food. I realise it's not the best selection for the vegans but you will have to bring your own bits or just have some chips. Oh, hold fire, I will organise a vegan pizza for everyone, I'm not a total bitch and if you want to eat rubber cheese, who am I to stop you? (I have never been good at cutting things out so I actually admire vegans. I was once told I should stop having dairy, for my skin. It lasted two days.)

All in all I want my funeral to be full of fun. Of course I need *some* crying, but that's why I've employed the wailers. It's a celebration, a time to get drunk for free and I will make sure it's worth the hangover. Irish funerals are known for being great fun and while, of course, they are sad at times, as soon as those sandwiches and drinks come out there's a smile on everyone's face.

Chapter Twenty-Two

Fantasy Future Plan

Planning into the future is a great thing just to help yourself aim high. Some people would consider that manifesting but I feel a bit unsure of the old manifestation game, I'm not one for journalling my everyday feelings. Nothing wrong if you do like a bit of a manifestation; it just doesn't work for me. What I do enjoy is reading about daily routines or, better still, watching them online. Some of the wilder ones suggest waking up at 4 a.m. and journalling for an hour. AN HOUR OF JOURNALLING! What on earth does anyone have to say so early in the morning and for that long? I consider myself a quick mover in the morning but even I couldn't do that. My sleep is so precious to me that I dread the mornings that I have to get up at six to film before the kids wake up; 4 a.m. is still the middle of the night for me.

I used to do a radio show which meant I would wake at 4.20 a.m. but after my nervous energy around being late diminished, my wake-up time extended to 4.40 a.m. and I always needed a half-hour nap when I got home. When I was pregnant it was a ninety-minute nap, which was so glorious, one of those naps where your face sticks to the pillow. Unless the kids wake me up or I have to work I would never ever get out of bed at 4 a.m., so journalling will have to wait until the fifth of never. I do fit a lot into my day but I am constantly rushing around like a blue-bottle and never finish everything I wanted to get done. By 6 p.m. I switch off completely and just about have enough energy to do the kids' bedtime and tidy up. By 7 p.m. it's woman down. This is why I get the fear when someone asks me to go out in the evening. It's very hard for me to be good fun after 7 p.m. so I have to resort to alcohol on those occasions. One day I will probably be queen of meditation and journalling but for now they're not even in my eyeline.

Rather than manifesting my life I like to think posi-tively about the future, putting good vibes and energy out there and hoping it gets reflected back. God laughs when you make plans but it's still important to have them in place and I like to curate my life as much as I can. (I feel like I talk about God a lot in this book and it's not because I'm a Holy Moly, it's just that He was such a huge part of our lives until we left mass that day with my twice-married mother.)

Okay, the fantasy future starts right here. I assume at some point my husband will come out as gay and then we really will be best friends. As far as I'm concerned there will never be enough gays in my life. Spenno will marry his partner in the most outrageous ceremony because he desperately wants it to be different to ours. Think Liberace meets Liza Minelli, who will also perform for their guests along with Steps and B'Witched. Spen's new husband is a total ride and also a fantastic cook. They move to New York and live in a big brownstone just across from Carrie Bradshaw's where I have my own quarters when I visit. When I'm there I spend my time wandering around the city spending money on some very outrageous clothes. (Gone are the days where I fill my Net-a-Porter basket and leave it to disappear – now I actually buy the stuff.)

Because I'll likely still enjoy working, I will start up a charity project of my own and treat it as an almost full-time job. Rescuing animals has become a big passion of mine and I've a huge farm in Howth where I mind them – an old folks' home for animals, although the odd puppy or kitten will slip in the net because how can anyone resist them? But the point of my rescue is that it has to be older animals that nobody wants. They'll live the dream and the live-in vet, who bears a striking resemblance to Bradley Cooper, will look after them (and me).

When I'm not at the rescue I'll be over in New York to spend time with Spencer and Toby (Spen's new husband) because their lives are so much fun. One night we all do edibles and I end up at one of their very high-end orgies in a lot of compromising positions. We all swear it will never happen again but it happens more often than not and half of them don't count anyway because I've blacked out from the edibles. Finally I'm riding rings around myself and have entered my slutty era at the grand age of fifty-six (a year after my facelift so I look amazing and am only with men under forty years of age). Sometimes the kids and I will join Spen and Toby and head off to Sitges in Spain. Spen is a very proud gay man and only wants to hang around the gays so we really do have a wonderful life.

My dream is to live in a big compound with my family and friends, kind of like a cult but without the mad shit that goes on. There's a man in Cork who bought a huge plot of land and built houses for his entire family and two best friends – that's what I would do if I won the Euromillions. There was a news story recently about seven Japanese best pals who bought a mansion together where they plan to retire and die. The place is enormous and I don't think they've thought through the stairs for when they're older, but otherwise they have the perfect plan. As I can't even organise a dinner with my pals this would take almost a lifetime for me to organise so I should probably get the ball rolling now!

Having never bought a Euromillions ticket in my entire life, yet still feeling disgruntled that I have never won it, I decide to buy one and win £250 million pounds. Thrilled, the first thing I buy is the commune for all my friends and family to live in. Next I buy myself a private jet ... I even use it to get to the shop down the road because I've still got that scabby bone in my body and have to make sure it gets the cost per wear. Taylor Swift never gets shit about her plane any more, because I use mine three times as much as she does so I take most of the heat.

My children will live in the commune I have created for us and will always want to spend time with me. It will be like a high-end resort with everything you need on site. Anything health-related will be there: saunas, ice baths and a huge gym (I'm sorry but this is my dream and I'm having the health retreat or it just wouldn't feel real). To balance it out there will be the unhealthy parts too that I will attend a lot more than usual because I have invented a hangover cure that works, it's how I made all of my money as well as a solution to anxiety. My kids are still my world and although I deeply miss them being babies and needing me more, they all have families of their own so that keeps me occupied.

All three of them have fantastic jobs. Gigi will be working for Chanel and gets a 50 per cent discount, which thrills me no end. T will be a zookeeper and at times brings home a baby lion and a penguin. Otto is a fantastic facialist and has kept me looking young for years. I have bought homes in New York, LA, a ski chalet, a house in Spain and just a humble abode in Paris. Eventually when I'm in LA hiking up Runyon canyon I meet a man. The man I meet is none other than Leonardo DiCaprio. He's a changed man and only wants to be with women who are over the age of fifty-five – myself and my new face have just about made the cut. He's also promised that headphones are a thing of the past and he's looking for his forever wife. He's quite disappointed when I say that I'm a polygamist but accepts that having part of me is better than nothing. I'm just not at a point in my life where I want to break up with Harry Styles and I'm certainly not willing to let go of my weekends with Brad Pitt and George Clooney – that's my favourite sandwich of the week!

All the moons and stars align when I turn sixty; I'm just not able to keep up with all of the gorgeous A-listers in my life so I retreat to a ranch – an exact copy of Ralph Lauren's ranch, because I'm simply too tired and not arsed to come up with my own ideas. All of a sudden I am living a very slow-paced life, but still with a lot of travelling because I have to get the use out of the PJ. Sometimes I just ask the pilot to fly around to nowhere in particular so I can enjoy the peace and quiet of the plane. Much to my relief someone has come up with a cure for death so I'm not going anywhere soon. I even get to bring some of my favourite people back from the dead such is the scientific nature of the cure. It has to be said they are a little tired and dusty-looking but Otto is so advanced in his career right now as a facialist that he makes them all sparkly and new. Somewhere along the line I decided to become a biohacker and with the advancements in that industry it now means I can drink tequila whenever I want, eat whatever I like and have the body of a sixteen-year-old. Life is just one big ball of fun. I'm feeling good and, more importantly, looking good. Surrounded by friends and family, we're enjoying ourselves no end because that's what life is all about; good people and all the craic!

Acknowledgements

Wow, that was a wild five months. I have spent every free moment writing to get this book completed and I have so many people to thank.

Firstly I would like to thank Spencer, my husband. I'm quite sure he got fed up with me telling him what I was writing, how many words I had written and how long I intended to write each day but he didn't show it. Spenny, you are very supportive and I have found such a great partner in you. I love our life together.

Theodore, Otto and Gigi you are my greatest achievements. I love watching you grow up and turn into the most charismatic and kind people. You always keep me on my toes with a few wobblers here and there, but for the most part you are MUCH better behaved than I ever was. Let's keep it that way.

Neil, you have been such an important part of our lives and I'm eternally grateful and equally shocked that you took the three of us on. You certainly didn't have it easy when we were young and, regardless of the stress you were put under, you always made sure we never noticed. I feel like my life wouldn't be as it is now had you not showed up for not only me, but my Mom as well. You continue to be such a huge influence in not just mine but all of our lives. We love you …

To my mom, Sandra, I understand there will be parts of this book you will skip through and well, to be honest. I'm hoping you'll skip through a good few chunks! I admire you so much for how you navigated what must have been a very difficult time. You always made us feel like things were totally fine and your strength was amazing. You are a fantastic mother and I am so grateful to be able to call you a friend after the years of torment you endured with me! You deserve all the happiness in the world and I love you so much.

Ambi Bambi my bestie for life and one of the most brilliant people I know. I think you're the absolute best, how lucky was I to get a sister like you. Also, how lucky were you to get a sister like me! We have been through half a lifetime together and there is plenty more fun to have.

To Winston and Bertie, the best dogs in the world, always around me when I was writing because I'm an oddball. Although I was mostly human-free during the writing of this book, I always had you two around. Until you started fighting or you started snoring, Bertie, so I had to kick you out of the room.

Louisa, we are quite the little team and I've loved growing my career alongside you. You always have my back and make sure that I can do the work that I do, as well as being able to spend lots of time with my kids. You get it, you work so hard and make things happen.

To Max, I forgot to thank you in my last book and there was no way I was forgetting again, seeing as you still go on about it. Great agent, great friend. Love you, Piggy.

To my whole family, there are far too many of you to mention but I got lucky with you loopers. I love that we are all so close.

To my dad, wherever you are we are always thinking of you. I'll never forget the fun times we had and will continue to have when we meet again.

There are so many producers and people I have to thank for my career, so many people took a chance on me and saw something in me, which means the world to me. I love this job, I love what I do and I never take it for granted.

To the team at HarperCollins and Ajda Vucicevic in particular, I've had such a brilliant time working with you. I have found a real love and passion for writing and don't plan on stopping any time soon. I appreciate you taking on this book and for all the help you have given.

To Nicky Lovick, thank you for helping me on this journey and continuing to do so.

To Oooooooooonie (Una McKevitt), who I love working with so much. Thank you for helping with the edit of this book, you are endlessly talented. Onto the next project, my friend ...

To everyone I work with in podcasting. It is something I never imagined I would love so much but I do. Part of that is getting to work with you. You're so good at what you do and it never feels like work when we are together.

To everyone who helps us at home, I am eternally grateful to you. I couldn't do what I do without you. Our kids are the most important thing in the world and knowing they are happy and safe when I'm at work means I can enjoy myself the way that I do.

To Marian Keyes and John Boyne, two of the greatest writers in the world, thank you for taking the time to read this book and give me quotes – it's one of the biggest pinch-me moments of my entire life. (I actually wanted to take my picture off the cover and just have the title with your quotes beside it, but my publisher declined.) Thank you both so, so much!